THE JEWISH STATE

by
Theodor Herzl

Dover Publications, Inc., New York

This Dover edition, first published in 1988, is an unabridged, unaltered republication of the work originally published in 1946 by the American Zionist Emergency Council, New York, based on a revised translation published by the Scopus Publishing Company, New York, 1943, which was, in turn, based on the first English-language edition, *A Jewish State,* translated by Sylvie d'Avigdor, and published by Nutt, London, England, 1896. The Herzl text was originally published under the title *Der Judenstaat* in Vienna, 1896. Please see the note on the facing page for further details.

Manufactured in the United States of America
Dover Publications, Inc.
31 East 2nd Street
Mineola, N.Y. 11501

Library of Congress Cataloging-in-Publication Data

Herzl, Theodor, 1860–1904.
   [Judenstaat. English]
   The Jewish state / by Theodor Herzl.
      p.   cm.
   Translation of: Judenstaat.
   Reprint. Originally published: New York : American Zionist Emergency Council, 1946.
   Bibliography: p.
   ISBN 0-486-25849-1 (pbk.)
   1. Zionism.   2. Herzl, Theodor, 1860–1904.   3. Zionists—Austria—Biography.
I. Title.
DS149.H514   1988
956.94'001—dc19   88-20374
                                                          CIP

"THE JEWISH STATE" is published by the American Zionist Emergency Council for its constituent organizations on the occasion of the 50th Anniversary of the publication of *"DER JUDENSTAAT"* in Vienna, February 14, 1896.

The translation of *"THE JEWISH STATE"* based on a revised translation published by the Scopus Publishing Company was further revised by Jacob M. Alkow, editor of this book. The biography was condensed from Alex Bein's *Theodor Herzl,* published by the Jewish Publication Society of America. The bibliography and the chronology were prepared by the Zionist Archives and Library. To Mr. Louis Lipsky and to all of the above mentioned contributors, the American Zionist Emergency Council is deeply indebted.

Contents

INTRODUCTION

by

Louis Lipsky

Introduction

Theodore Herzl was the first jew who projected the Jewish question as an international problem. "The Jewish State," written fifty years ago, was the first public expression, in a modern language, by a modern Jew, of a dynamic conception of how the solution of the problem could be accelerated and the ancient Jewish hope, slumbering in Jewish memory for two thousand years, could be fulfilled.

In 1882, Leo Pinsker, a Jewish physician of Odessa, disturbed by the pogroms of 1881, made a keen analysis of the position of the Jews, declared that anti-Semitism was a psychosis and incurable, that the cause of it was the abnormal condition of Jewish life, and that the only remedy for it was the removal of the cause through self-help and self-liberation. The Jewish people must become an independent nation, settled on the soil of their own land and leading the life of a normal people. Moses Hess in his "Rome and Jerusalem" classified the Jewish question as one of the nationalist struggles inspired by the French Revolution. Perez Smolenskin and E. Ben-Yehuda urged the revival of Hebrew and the resettlement of Palestine as the foundation for the rebirth of the Jewish people. Herzl was unaware of the existence of these works. His eyes were not directed to the problem in the same manner. When he wrote "The Jewish State" he was a journalist, living in Paris, sending his letters to the leading newspaper of Vienna, the *Neue Freie Presse,* and writing on a great variety of subjects. He was led to see Jewish life as a phenomenon in a changing world. He had adapted himself to a worldly outlook on all life. Through his efforts, the Jewish problem was raised to the higher

11

level of an international question which, in his judgment,
should be given consideration by enlightened statesmanship.
He was inspired to give his pamphlet a title that arrested
attention.

* * *

He wrote "The Jewish State" in a mood of restless agita-
tion. His ideas were thrown pell-mell into the white heat of
a spontaneous revelation. What was revealed dazzled and
blinded him. Alex Bein, in his excellent biography, gives an
intriguing description, drawn from Herzl's "Diaries," of
how "The Jewish State" was born. It was the revelation of
a mystic vision with flashes and overtones of prophecy. This
is what Bein says:

> "Then suddenly the storm breaks upon him. The
> clouds open. The thunder rolls. The lightning flashes
> about him. A thousand impressions beat upon him
> at the same time—a gigantic vision. He cannot
> think; he is unable to move; he can only write;
> breathless, unreflecting, unable to control himself
> or to exercise his critical faculties lest he dam the
> eruption, he dashes down his thoughts on scraps of
> paper—walking, standing, lying down, on the street,
> at the table, in the night—as if under unceasing
> command. So furiously did the cataract of his
> thoughts rush through him, that he thought he was
> going out of his mind. He was not working out the
> idea. The idea was working him out. It would have
> been an hallucination had it not been so informed by
> reason from first to last."

Not only did the Magic Title evoke a widespread interest
among the intellectuals of the day, but it brought Jews out

of the ghettos and made them conscious of their origin and destiny. It made them feel that there was a world that might be won for their cause, hitherto never communicated to strangers. Through Herzl, Jews were taught not to fear the consequences of an international movement to demand their national freedom. Thereafter, with freedom, they were to speak of a Zionist Congress, of national funds, of national schools, of a flag and a national anthem, and the redemption of their land. Their spirits were liberated and in thought they no longer lived in ghettos. Herzl taught them not to hide in corners. At the First Congress he said, "We have nothing to do with conspiracy, secret intervention or indirect methods. We wish to put the question in the arena and under the control of free public opinion." The Jews were to be active factors in their emancipation and, if they wished it, what was described in "The Jewish State" would not be a dream but a reality.

* * *

The beginnings of the Jewish renaissance preceded the appearance of "The Jewish State" by several decades. In every section of Russian Jewry and extending to wherever the Jews clung to their Hebraic heritage, there was an active Zionist life. The reborn Hebrew was becoming an all-pervading influence. There were scores of Hebrew schools and academies. Hebrew journals of superior quality had a wide circulation. Ever since the pogroms of 1881, the ideas of Pinsker and Smolenskin and Gordon were discussed with great interest and deep understanding. There were many Zionist societies in Russia, in Poland, in Rumania, in Galicia and even in the United States. In "The Jewish State" Herzl alludes to the language of The Jewish State and passes Hebrew by as a manifestation of no great significance. He has a poorer opinion of Yiddish, the common language of

Jews, which he regards as "the furtive language of prisoners." This was obviously an oversight. With the advent
of Herzl, however, Zionism was no more a matter of domestic concern only. It was no longer an internal Jewish
problem only, not a theme for discussion only at Zionist
meetings, not a problem to heat the spirits of Jewish writers.
The problem of Jewish exile now occupied a place on the
agenda of international affairs.

* * *

Herzl was not so distant from his people as many of the
Russian Zionists at first surmised. He was familiar with the
social anti-Semitism of Austria and Germany. He knew of
the disabilities of the Jews in Russia. There are many references in his feuilletons to matters of Jewish interest. He had
read an anti-Semitic book written by Eugen Duhring called
"The Jewish Problem as a Problem of Race, Morals and
Culture." One of his closest friends had gone to Brazil for
a Jewish committee to investigate the possibility of settling
Jews in that part of South America. In 1892 he wrote an
article on French anti-Semitism in which he considered the
solution of a return to Zion and seemed to reject it. He
wrote "The New Ghetto" two years before "The Jewish
State" appeared. He was present at the trial of Alfred Dreyfus in December, 1894. He witnessed the degradation of
Dreyfus and heard the cries of "Down with the Jews" in the
streets of Paris. He read Edouard Drumont's anti-Semitic
journal "La France Juive" and said, "I have to thank Drumont for much of the freedom of my present conception of
the Jewish problem." While he was in Paris he was stirred
as never before by the feeling that the plight of the Jews
was a problem which would have to have the cooperation of
enlightened statesmanship. What excited him in the stran-

gest way was the unaccountable indifference of Jews themselves to what seemed to him the menace of the existing situation. He saw the Jews in every land encircled by enemies, hostility to them growing with the increase of their numbers. In his excitement he thought first of Jewish philanthropists. He sought an interview with Baron Maurice de Hirsch in May, 1895. He planned an address to the Rothschilds. He talked of his ideas to friends in literary circles. His mind was obsessed by a gigantic problem which gave him no rest. He was struggling to pierce the veils of revelation. He saw a world in which the Jewish people lacked a fulcrum for national action and therefore had to seek to create it through beneficence. He had a remarkably resourceful and agile imagination. He weighed ideas, balanced them, discarded them, reflected, reconsidered, tried to reconcile contradictions, and finally came to what seemed to him at the moment the synthesis of the issue which seemed acceptable to reason and sentiment.

* * *

Obviously, "The Jewish State" was not a dogmatic finality. Most of the plans for settlement and migration are improvisations. The pamphlet was not a rigid plan or a blueprint. It was not a description of a Utopia, although some parts of it give that impression. It had an indicated destiny but was not bound by a rigid line. It was the illumination of a dynamic thought and followed the light with the hope that it might lead to fulfillment. There was room for detours and variations. It was to be rewritten, as he knew, not by its author but by the Jewish people on their way to freedom.

* * *

In fact, it was revised from the moment the Zionist movement was organized on an international basis. The "Society of Jews" became the Zionist Organization, with its statutes, its procedures, its public excitement and controversies. "The Jewish Company" became the Bank; then more specifically, the Jewish Colonial Trust and later the Anglo-Palestine Bank. The description of the *Gestor*, which appears in the final chapter of the pamphlet, was never referred to again, but in effect it was incorporated in the idea of a state in-the-process-of-becoming. Its legitimate successor is the Jewish Agency referred to in the Mandate for Palestine. He was first led by the idea that the way to the charter was through the Sultan and that the Sultan would be influenced by Kaiser Wilhelm. But both princes failing him, he turned to England and Joseph Chamberlain, and came to the Uganda proposal. This was Herzl's one political success although the project was, in effect, rejected by the Zionist Congress. But this encounter with England was a precedent which led to much speculation in Zionist circles and gave a turn to Zionist thought away from Germany and Turkey. It served to inspire Dr. Chaim Weizman to make his home in England with the express purpose of seeking English sympathy for the Zionist ideal. The successor of Joseph Chamberlain was Arthur James Balfour. When Herzl opened Chamberlain's door, Zionism had an easier access to the England of Balfour.

When Herzl first appeared on the political scene, he thought of courtiers and statesmen, of princes and kings. He found that they could not be relied upon for truth or stability. They were encircled by favorites and mercenaries. Enormous responsibilities rested upon their shoulders but they seemed to behave with regard to these responsibilities as if they were gamblers or amateurs. Herzl soon realized that these were frail reeds that would break under the slightest pressure. He came to put his trust in the Jewish people, the only real source of strength for the purpose of redemption. Confidence in themselves would give them power to breach their prison walls. His aristocratic republic had to become a movement of democracy. Only in "The Jewish State" will you find reference to a movement based upon Jews who endorse a "fixed program," and then become members under the "discipline" of leadership. When Herzl faced the First Congress, he saw that this conception of Zionism was foreign to the nature and character of the Jewish people. The shekel was the registry of a name. It led the way to the elevation of the individual in Zionist affairs, first as a member of a democratic army "willing" the fulfillment, and then settling in Palestine to become the hands that built the Homeland.

Arrayed in the armor of democracy, the Zionist movement made the self-emancipation ideal of Pinsker live in the soul of Herzl. At a number of Congresses, in his articles in Die Welt, Herzl showed how that idea had become an integral part of his life, although his first thoughts ran in quite another direction.

But his analysis of anti-Semitism and how to approach the problem remains true today after Hitler, as it was true then after Dreyfus. This was the authentic revelation that in his last days was fixed in his mind. The homelessness of the Jewish people must come to an end. That tragedy is a world problem. It is to be solved by world statesmanship in cooperation with the reawakened Jewish people. It is to be solved by the establishment of a free Jewish State in their historic Homeland. Herzl manifested his utter identification with the destiny of his own people at the Uganda Congress when he faced the rebellious Russian Zionists, spoke words of consolation to them and gave them assurances of his fealty to Zion. He died a few months later.

"The Jewish State" was not regarded by Herzl as a piece of literature. It was a political document. It was to serve as the introduction to political action. It was to lead to the conversion of leaders in political life. It was to win converts to the idea of a Jewish State. Although a shy man at first, he did not hesitate to make his way through the corridors of the great and suffer the humiliations of the suppliant. Through that remarkable friend and Christian, the Reverend William H. Hechler, he met the Grand Duke of Baden; he made the rounds of German statesmen, Count zu Eulenburg, Foreign Minister, Von Buelow and Reichschancellor Hohenlohe; then he met the favorites who encircled Sultan Abdul Hamid and the Sultan himself. He placed the dramatic personae of his drama on the stage. The plan involved the Turkish debt, the German interest in the Orient. It involved stimulating the Russians and visiting the Pope. At first his political activities were conducted as the author of a startling pamphlet, then as the leader of his people. He became conscious of his leadership, and played his part with superb dignity. He had ease of manner and correct form. He created the impression of a regal personality; his noble appearance hid his hesitations and fears. With the Sultan he played the most remarkable game of diplomacy. He believed that once a mutual interest could be arrived at, he would be able to secure the funds, although at the time of speaking he had no funds at all. Adjusting himself to the wily Turk, he had to change and diminish his demands and finally, when he was dangerously near a disclosure, he was saved by the Sultan's transferring his interest to the French and obtaining his funds from them. With Kaiser Wilhelm, he soon appreciated the fact that he had to deal with a great theatrical personality who spoke of plans and purpose with great fire, but had no courage and whose convictions melted away in the face of obstacles.

The world Herzl dealt with has passed away. The Turkish Empire now occupies a small part of the Near East. Its former provinces have now become "sovereign" states struggling to establish harmony between themselves and feeding on their animus towards the Jewish people returning home. The methods of diplomacy have changed. Loudness of speech is no longer out of order. Frankness and brutality may be expected at any international gathering. It is now felt as never before that behind political leaders, rulers, princes, statesmen, the people are advancing and soon will be able to push aside those who make of the relations of peoples a game and a gamble, a struggle for power, which, when achieved, dissolves into the nothingness of vanity.

* * *

"The Jewish State" should be regarded as one of a series of books, variations on the same theme, composed by the same author. The first was "The New Ghetto" (1894). That was a play which dealt with the social life of the upper class of Jews in Vienna. Then came the "Address to the Rothschilds." That was a memorandum which contained a proposal to Jewish philanthropists. "The Jewish State" was the third effort of an agitated mind, wavering between the projection of a Utopia or a thesis, and containing the political solution of the Jewish problem. The final variant of the original theme was the novel "Altneuland." Here he pictured the Promised Land as it might become twenty years after the beginning of the Zionist movement. In the interims, he played on the exciting stage of the Zionist Congresses. He paid court to princes and their satellites. He led in the organization of the Jewish Colonial Trust and the Jewish National

Fund. He delivered political addresses and engaged in political controversy. He began the writing of his "Diaries" after he had written "The Jewish State." His whole personality is reflected in that remarkable book. There you see his ideas in the process of becoming clear. There you see his sharp reactions; the reflection of his hopes, his disappointments, his shifts from untenable positions to positions possible after defeat. There you read his penetrating analysis of the figures on the Zionist stage upon whom he had to rely. There you are made to feel his doubts, his dread of death. In the midst of life he felt himself encircled by the Shadow of Death. There you found the explanation of his great haste, why he was so anxious to bring a measure of practical reality to the Jewish people even if it necessitated a detour from the land which was becoming more and more a part of his hopes and desires. The "Diaries" are unrestrained and unstudied. They were written hurriedly in the heat of the moment. They reveal the making of the great personality who gave only a glimpse of himself in "The Jewish State." They show the writer evolving as the hero of a great and lasting legend. The pamphlet is one of the chapters in the story of his struggle to achieve in eight years what his people had not been able to achieve in two thousand years. He gave his life to write it.

Theodor Herzl

A BIOGRAPHY
based on the work of

Alex Bein

THEODOR HERZL WAS BORN ON WEDNESDAY, MAY 2, 1860.
in the city of Budapest.

Almost next door to his father's house was the liberal-reform temple. To this house of worship the little boy went regularly with his father on Sabbaths and Holy Days. At home, too, the essentials of the ritual were observed. One ceremony which Theodor learned in childhood remained with him; before every important event and decision he sought the blessing of his parents.

Even stronger than these impressions, however, was the influence of his mother. Her education had been German through and through; there was not a day on which she did not slip into German literature, especially the classics.

The Jewish world, not alien to her, did not find expression through her; her conscious efforts were all directed toward implanting the German cultural heritage in her children. Of even deeper significance was her sympathetic attitude toward the pride which showed early in her son, and her skill in transferring to him her sense of form, of bearing, of tactfulness and of simple grace.

At about the age of twelve he read in a German book about the Messiah-King whom many Jews still awaited and who would come riding, like the poorest of the poor on an ass. The history of the Exodus and the legend of the liberation by the King-Messiah ran together in the boy's mind, inspiring in him the theme of a wonderful story which he sought in vain to put into literary form.

A little while thereafter Herzl had the following dream: "The King-Messiah came, a glorious and majestic old man, took me in his arms, and swept off with me on the

wings of the wind. On one of the iridescent clouds we
encountered the figure of Moses. The features were those
familiar to me out of my childhood in the statue by
Michelangelo. The Messiah called to Moses: It is for this
child that I have prayed. But to me he said: Go, declare
to the Jews that I shall come soon and perform great wonders and great deeds for my people and for the whole
world."

It may be to this period (of his *Bar Mitzvah*) of reawakened Jewish sensitivity, of heightened responsiveness to the
expectations of his elders, of resurgent interest in Jewish
historical studies—it may be to this period that the dream
of a dedicated life belonged. It is almost certain, too, that
for the great event of the *Bar Mitzvah* the old grandfather
of Semlin came to Pest. About this time, again, Alkalai,
that early, all-but-forgotten Zionist, passed through Vienna
and Budapest on his final journey to Palestine. Whether
or not each one of these circumstances had a direct effect
on the boy, the whole complex surrounds his *Bar Mitzvah*
with the suggestion of the mission of his life, and, certainly,
occasion was given for the awakening in him of the feeling
of dedication to a great enterprise.

The attention, energy and time which Herzl devoted to
literature, at fifteen, his absorption in himself, his activity
in the school literary society meant of course so much less
given to his school work. He found no time at all for science;
Jewish questions likewise disappeared from his interests; he
was completely absorbed by German literary culture. This is
all the more astonishing when we reflect that anti-Semitism
continued to increase steadily. As a grown man Herzl could
recall that one of his teachers, in defining the word
"heathen," had said, "such as idolators, Mohammedans and
Jews." Whether it was this incident,—as the memory of

the grown man always insisted—which enraged him beyond endurance, or the increasingly bad school reports, or both circumstances together, the fact remains that on February 4, 1875 Herzl left the Technical School.

At sixteen to eighteen in High School, he struggled to define the basic principles of various literary art forms in order that he might see more clearly what he himself wanted to say. He took an active and eager part in the work of the "German Self-Education Society" created by the students of his school. The Jewish world, whose inferior position always wounded his pride, and whose obstinate separatism seemed to him utterly meaningless, drifted further and further out of his mind.

At eighteen, after the sudden death of his only sister, the family moved to Vienna where Herzl entered the University as a law student. Herzl, who accounted himself a liberal and an Austrian patriot, plunged eagerly into the activities of a large student Cultural Association, attended its discussions and directed its literary evenings. He had occasion, there, to deride certain Jewish fellow members who, in his view, displayed an excessive eagerness in their loyalty to various movements.

This was the extent to which, in these days, he occupied himself with the Jewish question—at least externally. He concerned himself little or not at all with the official Jewish world which was seeking to submerge itself in the surrounding world. He seldom visited the synagogue.

He was an omnivorous reader. His extraordinary knowledge of books was evident in his conversation, for he liked to adorn his speech with quotations, which came readily to his memory. Herzl read Eugen Dühring's book *The Jewish Problem as a Problem of Race, Morals and Culture*—the first and most important effort to find a "scientific," philosophic, biologic and historical basis for the anti-Semitism which was sweeping through Europe in those days (1881). Dühring saw the Jewish question as a purely racial question, and for him the Jewish race was without any worth whatsoever. Those peoples which, out of a false sentiment of humanity, had permitted the Jews to live among them with equal and sometimes even with superior rights, had to be liberated from the harmful intruder, had to be de-Judaized.

The reading of this book had the effect upon him of a blow between the eyes. The observations set down in his diary burn with indignation: "An infamous book . . . If Dühring, who unites so much undeniable intelligence with so much universality of knowledge, can write like this, what are we to expect from the ignorant masses?"

This passionate reaction to Dühring's book shows us how deeply he had been moved, and how fearfully he had been shaken in his belief that the Jewish question was on the point of disappearing. We shall find echoes of this experience in the pages of the *Judenstaat*. For the time being, however, he shrank from the logical consequences of his reactions. His inner pride began to build itself up.

The more immediate reaction was undoubtedly a sharpened perception and evaluation of his fellow-members in the Fraternity. Herzl had joined and been active in a duelling Fraternity. Here, too, anti-Semitism was breaking through; student after student expressed himself favorably toward the Jew-baiting speeches of Schoenerer, who was making a special effort to win over the universities. In the Fraternity debates Herzl expressed himself sharply against any open or covert manifestation of such sympathy. But he was already known for the sharpness of his tongue and the individuality of his views. Thus he won to himself neither the few co-religionists who belonged to the Fraternity nor the mass of the Germanic students.

He had learned from newspaper reports that the Wagner Memorial meeting, in which his Fraternity had taken a part, had been transformed into an anti-Semitic demonstration. His Fraternity had, therefore, identified itself with a movement which he, as a believer in liberty, was bound to condemn, even if he had not been a Jew. "It is pretty clear that, handicapped as I am by my Semitism (the word was not yet known at the time of my entry), I would today refrain from seeking a membership which would, indeed, probably be refused me; it must also be clear to every decent person that under these circumstances I cannot wish to retain my membership." Herzl withdrew from the organization.

On July 30, 1884, Herzl was admitted to the bar in Vienna. His student days were over. A new era opened for him, with its challenge to prove whether or not there was something in him to establish and proclaim to the world.

In August, he entered on his law practice in the service of the state and was soon transferred to the court of Salzburg. Though he may at that time have been so far from Judaism that only pride and a decent respect for the feelings of his parents stood between him and baptism, he could not help perceiving that as a Jew he would find the higher levels of the civil service hierarchy closed to him. On August 5, 1885, he withdrew from the service, determined to seek fame and fortune as a writer.

Brimming with hope, he set out on a journey which was to be the introduction to his literary life. He visited Belgium and Holland and in Berlin made valuable connections and became a regular contributor to several important newspapers. Thus the range of his connections and relationships widened from year to year, and when he travelled again it was an ever-widening audience that waited for his impressions and observations.

In a book of reprinted feuilletons of Herzl which appeared in the first years of his success as a journalist a total of seven or eight lines is devoted to Jews. His impressions of the Ghetto in Rome. "What a steaming in the air, what a street! Countless open doors and windows thronged with innumerable pallid and worn-out faces. The ghetto! With what base and persistent hatred these unfortunates have been persecuted for the sole crime of faithfulness to their religion. We've travelled a long way since those times: nowadays the Jew is despised only for having a crooked nose, or for being a plutocrat even when he happens to be a pauper." Pity and bitterness abound in these lines, but they are written by a detached spectator. He did not know how much of the Jew there was in him even in this feeling of remoteness from a world which offered him not living reality but folly.

By 1892, Herzl had achieved great success as a dramatist and as a journalist; his plays had been performed on the stage of the leading theatre of Vienna and, to cap the climax, came an appointment to the staff of the *Neue Freie Presse*, one of the most distinguished papers on the continent.

Early in October he received a telegram from the *Neue Freie Presse* asking whether he would accept the post of Paris correspondent. He replied at once in the affirmative, and proceeded to the French capital at the end of the same month. He wrote to his parents: "The position of Paris correspondent is the springboard to great things, and I shall achieve them, to your great joy, my dear beloved parents."

Herzl sustained successfully the comparison with his great models and predecessors. In style as well as in substance his reports and articles were masterpieces of their kind. He came to his task with the equipment of a perfect feuilletonist; his style was polished and musical; he possessed in an exceptional degree the capacity to describe natural scenery in a few fine clear strokes and of hinting at, rather than of reproducing, a mood with a minimum of language. Everything was there, background, mood and development of action in plastic balance. It was only now, when a great opportunity provoked him to the highest effort, that all the lessons of the years of his apprenticeship built up a many-sided perfection.

He threw himself seriously and diligently into the journalistic craft. He observed with close attention all that went on about him, and listened with sharpened ears. But the moment had not yet come for the unveiling of a mission within him. He was on the way; the process of preparation had begun.

How, in this mood of his, could he possibly have avoided clashing with the Jewish question? As far back as the time of his Spanish journey, when he had sought healing from his domestic and spiritual torments, the question had presented itself to him and had cried for artistic expression. His call to Paris had been a welcome pretext, perhaps, putting off the writing of his Jewish novel—the more so as he probably was not ripe enough for such an undertaking. Now that he was in Paris, where his eyes were opened to the full range of the social process, he began to draw nearer in spirit to his fellow-Jews, and to look upon them more warmly and with less inhibition. He found them as difficult aesthetically as before, but he tried hard to grasp the essence of their character and substance, and to judge them without prejudice.

When Herzl arrived in Paris anti-Semitism, had not—

in spite of Drumont's exertions, and in spite of his paper, *la Libre Parole,* founded in 1892—achieved the dimensions of a genuine movement, nor was it destined to become one in the German sense. But it served as the focus for all kinds of discontents and resentments; it attracted certain serious critical spirits, too; its influence grew from day to day, and the position of the Jews became increasingly uncomfortable.

Herzl's contact with anti-Semitism dated back to his student days, when it had first taken on the form of a social political movement. He had been aware of it as a writer, though the contact had never ripened into a serious inner struggle or compelled him to give utterance to it.

Now he read Drumont, as he had read Dühring. The impression was again a profound one. What moved him most in the work was the totality of a world picture based on a considered hostility to the Jews.

A ritual-murder trial was in progress in the town of Xanten, in the Rhineland. On August 31, 1892, Herzl, dealing with this subject as with all other subjects of public interest, summed up the general situation in a long report entitled "French anti-Semitism."

By now Herzl was no longer content with a simple acceptance of the facts; he was looking for the deeper significance of the universal enmity directed against the Jews. For the world it is a lightning conductor. But so far it was only a flash of insight which ended in nothing more than a literary paradox. However, from now on it gave him no peace.

At the turn of the year 1892-93 there came a sharp clarification in his ideas. He had followed closely the evasive debates in the Austrian Reichstag—debates which forever dodged the reality by turning the question into one of religion. "It is no longer—and it has not been for a long time—a theological matter. It has nothing whatsoever to do with religion and conscience," declared Herzl. "What is more, everyone knows it. The Jewish question is neither nationalistic nor religious. It is a social question."

Then came the summer, 1894, and at its close Herzl took a much needed vacation. He spent the month of September in Baden, near Vienna, in the company of his fellow-feuilletonist on the *Neue Freie Presse*, Ludwig Speidel. Herzl has left a record of their conversation. What he gave Speidel was more or less what he had felt, many years before, after his reading of Dühring. He admitted the substance of the anti-Semitic accusation which linked the Jew with money; he defended the Jew as the victim of a long historic process for which the Jew was not responsible. "It is not our fault, not the fault of the Jews, that we find ourselves forced into the role of alien bodies in the midst of various nations. The ghetto, which was not of our making, bred in us certain anti-social qualities . . . Our original character cannot have been other than magnificent and proud; we were men who knew how to face war and how to defend the state; had we not started out with such gifts, how could we have survived two thousand years of unrelenting persecution?"

At that time Herzl came across the Zionist solution, and definitely rejected it. Discussing the novel *Femme de Claude*, by Dumas the younger, he says of one of its characters: "The good Jew Daniel wants to rediscover the homeland of his race and gather his scattered brothers into it. But a man like Daniel would surely know that the historic homeland of the Jews no longer has any value for them. It is childish to go in search of the geographic location of this homeland. And if the Jews really 'returned home' one day, they would discover on the next day that they do not belong together. For centuries they have been rooted in diverse nationalisms; they differ from each other, group by group; the only thing they have in common is the pressure which holds them together. All humiliated peoples have Jewish characteristics, and as soon as the pressure is removed they react like liberated men."

The inner apotheosis was drawing nearer and nearer for Herzl. In October, 1894, Herzl was in the studio of the sculptor, Samuel Friedrich Beer, who was making a bust of him. The conversation turned to the Jewish question and to the growth of the anti-Semitic movement in Vienna, the hometown of both Herzl and Beer. It was useless for the Jew to turn artist and to dissociate himself from money, said Herzl. "The blot sticks. We can't break away from the ghetto." A great excitement seized Herzl, and he left the atelier, and on the way home the inspiration came on him like a hammerblow. What was it? The complete outline of a play, "like a block of basalt."

With this play Herzl completed his inner return to his people. Until then, with all his emotional involvement in the question, he had stood outside it as the observer, the student, the clarifier, or even the defender. He had provided the world-historic background for the problem, he had diagnosed it and given the prognosis for the future. Now he was immersed in it and identified with it.

He had become its spokesman and attorney, as he was spokesman and attorney for other victims of injustice. It was no accident that the hero of the play was a lawyer by vocation and avocation. For the hero was Herzl himself, and the transformation which unfolded in Dr. Jacob Samuel was the transformation which was unfolding in Theodore Herzl.

He belongs utterly to the Jews; it is for them that he fights, and, dying, he still sees himself as the fighter for their future. What future Jacob Samuel foresaw for the Jews in his dying moments remained unclear. It would appear that Herzl himself still believed that a deepening of mutual understanding between Jews and non-Jews might bring the solution.

But Herzl had travelled so much further by this time that he could not have in mind the "reconciliation" which would come by the capitulation of baptism. Indeed, the play emphasizes as a first prerequisite in human relations the element of self-respect. "If you become untrue to yourself," says the clever mother to the son, in the play, "you musn't complain if others become untrue to you." It was like a fresh wind blowing suddenly through the choking atmosphere of a lightless room. It was a new attitude: decent pride!

It called for a frightful effort to descend from the intoxicating heights of creativity to the ordinary round of work. For weeks now his regular employment had filled Herzl with revulsion. The first reports of the Dreyfus trial, which appeared while he was working on his *New Ghetto*, therefore made no particular impression on him. It looked like a sordid espionage affair in which a foreign power—before long it was revealed that the foreign power was Germany, acting through Major von Schwartzkoppen— had been buying up through its agent secret documents of the French general staff. An officer by the name of Alfred Dreyfus was named as the culprit, and no one had reason to doubt that he was guilty, even though Drumont's *Libre Parole* was exploiting the fact that the man was a Jew.

But, after the degradation of Dreyfus, Herzl became more and more convinced of his innocence. "A Jew who, as an officer on the general staff, has before him an honorable

career, cannot commit such a crime . . . The Jews, who
have so long been condemned to a state of civic dishonor,
have, as a result, developed an almost pathological hunger
for honor, and a Jewish officer is in this respect specifically
Jewish."

"The Dreyfus case," he wrote in 1899, "embodies more
than a judicial error; it embodies the desire of the vast
majority of the French to condemn a Jew, and to condemn
all Jews in this one Jew. Death to the Jews! howled the mob,
as the decorations were being ripped from the captain's coat
. . . Where? In France. In republican, modern, civilized
France, a hundred years after the Declaration of the Rights
of Man. The French people, or at any rate the greater part
of the French people, does not want to extend the rights
of man to Jews. The edict of the great Revolution had
been revoked."

Illumined thus in retrospect, the "curious excitement"
which gripped Herzl on that occasion takes on a special
significance. "Until that time most of us believed that the
solution of the Jewish question was to be patiently waited
for as part of the general development of mankind. But
when a people which in every other respect is so progressive
and so highly civilized can take such a turn, what are we
to expect from other peoples, which have not even attained
the level which France attained a hundred years ago?"

In that fateful moment, when he heard the howling of
the mob outside the gates of the *Ecole Militaire,* the realization flashed upon Herzl that anti-Semitism was deep-rooted
in the heart of the people—so deep, indeed, that it was
impossible to hope for its disappearance within a measurable
period of time. Precisely because he was so sensitive to
his honor as a Jew, precisely because he had proclaimed,
in the *New Ghetto,* the ideal of human reconciliation, and

had taken the ultimate decision to stand by his Jewishness, the ghastly spectacle of that winter morning must have shaken him to the depths of his being. It was as if the ground had been cut away from under his feet. In this sense Herzl could say later that the Dreyfus affair had made him a Zionist.

He saw all about him the ever fiercer light of a blazing anti-Semitism. In the French Chamber of Deputies the deputy Denis made an interpellation on the influence of the Jews in the political administration of the country. In Vienna a Jewish member of the Reichstag rose to speak and was howled down. On April 2, 1895, were held the municipal elections of Vienna, and there was an enormous increase in the number of anti-Semitic aldermen. Changing plans passed tumultuously through his mind. He wanted to write a book on "The Condition of the Jews," consisting of reports on all the important Jewish colonization enterprises in Russia, Galicia, Hungary, Bohemia, the Orient, and those more recently founded in Palestine, about which he had heard from a relative. Alphonse Daudet, the famous French author with whom he had discussed the whole matter, felt that Herzl ought to write a novel; it would carry further than a play. "Look at *Uncle Tom's Cabin.*"

He returned to his former plan of a Jewish novel which he had abandoned when he was called to his assignment on the *Neue Freie Presse* in Paris. His friend Kana, the suicide, was no longer to be the central figure. He was instead to be "the weaker one, the beloved friend of the hero," and would take his own life after a series of misfortunes, while the Promised Land was being discovered or rather founded. When the hero aboard the ship which was taking him to the Promised Land would receive the moving farewell letter of his friend, his first reaction after his horror would be one of rage: "Idiot! Fool! Miserable hopeless weakling! A life lost which belonged to us!"

We can see the Zionist idea arising. Its outlines are still indefinite, but the decisive idea is clearly visible; only by migration can this upright human type be given its chance to emerge. In *The New Ghetto* Jacob Samuel is a hero because he knows how to choose an honorable death. Now the death of a useful man is criminally wasteful. For there are great tasks to be undertaken.

In essence it is the Act and not the Word that confronts us. What last impulse it was that actually carried Herzl from the Word to the Act it will be difficult to tell—he himself could not have given the answer. Little things may play a dramatic role not less effectively than great ones when a man is so charged with purpose as Herzl then was.

In the early days of May, Herzl addressed to Baron de Hirsch (the sponsor of Jewish colonization in Argentina), the letter which opens his Jewish political career. His request for an interview was granted. Herzl prepared an outline of his position in notes, lest he omit something important during their conversation.

In these notes he writes: "If the Jews are to be transformed into men of character in a reasonable period of time, say ten or twenty years, or even forty—the interval needed by Moses—it cannot be done without migration. Who is going to decide whether conditions are bad enough today to warrant our migration? And whether the situation is hopeless? And the Congress which you (i.e. Hirsch) have convened for the first of August in a hotel in Switzerland? You will preside over this Congress of notables. Your call will be heard and answered in every part of the world.

"And what will be the message given to the men assembled? 'You are pariahs! You must forever tremble at the thought that you are about to be deprived of your rights and stripped of your possessions. You will be insulted when you walk in the street. If you are poor, you suffer doubly. If you are rich, you must conceal the fact. You are not admitted to any honorable calling, and if you deal in money you are made the special focus of contempt . . . The situation will not change for the better, but rather for the worse . . . There is only way out: into the Promised Land.' "

Where the Promised Land was to be located, how it was to be acquired, is not yet mentioned. Herzl does not seem to have thought this question of decisive significance; it was a scientific matter. It was the organization of the migration which held his attention, the political preparations among the Powers, the preliminary changes to be brought about among the masses by training, by "tremendous propaganda, the popularization of the idea through newspapers, books, pamphlets, lectures, pictures, songs."

On the day of his conversation with Baron de Hirsch, Herzl wrote him a long letter in which he sought to supplement the information and impressions which had been the result of the meeting. "Please believe me, the political life of an entire people—particularly when that people is scattered throughout the entire world—can be set in motion only with imponderables floating high in the air. Do you know what the German Reich sprang from? From dreams, songs, fantasies, and gold-black bands worn by students. And that in a brief period of time. What? You do not understand imponderables? And what is religion? Bethink yourself what the Jews have endured for two thousand years for the sake of this fantasy . . .

"The exodus to the Promised Land presents itself as a tremendous enterprise in transportation, unparalleled in the modern world. What transportation? It is a complex of all human enterprises which we shall fit into each other like cog-wheels. And in the very first stages of the enterprise we shall find employment for the ambitious younger masses of our people: all the engineers, architects, technologists, chemists, doctors, and lawyers, those who have emerged in the last thirty years from the ghetto and who have been moved by the faith that they can win their bread and a little honor outside the framework of our Jewish business futilities. Today they must be filled with despair, they constitute the foundation of a frightful over-educated proletariat. But it is to these that all my love belongs, and I am just as set on increasing their number as you are set on diminishing it. It is in them that I perceive the latent power of the Jewish people. In brief, my kind."

In this letter of June 3, 1895, Herzl for the first time imparted his new Jewish policy to a stranger. The writing down of his views, as well as his conversation on the subject, had had a stronger effect on himself than on Hirsch. He had obtained a clear vision of the new and revolutionary character of his proposals. On the same day or shortly thereafter he began a diary under the title of *The Jewish Question.*

"For some time now, I have been engaged upon a work of indescribable greatness. I do not know yet whether I shall carry it through. It has assumed the aspect of some mighty dream. But days and weeks have passed since it has filled me utterly, it has overflown into my unconscious self, it accompanies me wherever I go, it broods above all my commonplace conversation, it peeps over my shoulder at the comical little journalistic work which I must carry out. It disturbs and intoxicates me."

Then suddenly the storm breaks upon him. The clouds open, the thunder rolls and the lightning flashes about him.

A thousand impressions beat upon him simultaneously, a gigantic vision. He cannot think, he cannot act, he can only write; breathless, unreflecting, unable to control himself, unable to exercise the critical faculty lest he dam the eruption, he dashes down his thoughts on scraps of paper— "Walking, standing, lying down, in the street, at table, in the night," as if under unceasing command.

And then doubts rise up from the depths. He dines with well-to-do, educated, oppressed people who confront the question of anti-Semitism in a state of complete helplessness: "They do not suspect it, but they are ghetto-natures, quiet, decent, timid. That is what most of us are. Will they understand the call to freedom and to manhood? When I left them my spirits were very low. Again, my plan appeared to me to be crazy." Then at once he comes to "Today I am again as firm as steel." He notes the next morning. "The flabbiness of the people I met yesterday gives me all the more grounds for action."

Clearer and clearer becomes the picture which he has of himself and of his task in the history of his people. "I picked up once again the torn thread of the tradition of our people. I lead it into the Promised Land."

"The Promised Land, where we can have hooked noses, black or red beards, and bow legs, without being despised for it; where we can live at last as free men on our own soil, and where we can die peacefully in our own fatherland. There we can expect the award of honor for great deeds, so that the offensive cry of 'Jew!' may become an honorable appellation, like German, Englishman, Frenchman—in brief, like all civilized peoples; so that we may be able to form our state to educate our people for the tasks which at present still lie beyond our vision. For surely God would not have kept us alive so long if there were not assigned to us a specific role in the history of mankind." He adds: "The Jewish state is a world need." He draws the logical consequence for himself: "I believe that for me life has ended and world history begun."

He let the first storm pass over him, yielding to its imperious will, making no effort to stem its fury lest he interrupt the inspiration. When it had had its way with him, he took hold of himself again, and gathered up his energies for the effort to reconstruct everything logically and in ordered fashion. He was afraid that death might come upon him before he had succeeded in reducing to transferable form his historic vision. Thus, in the course of five days, he added to his diary a sixty-five page pamphlet—in effect the outline of *Der Judenstaat*—which he called: *Address to the Rothschilds.*

In the address he writes, "I have the solution to the Jewish question. I know it sounds mad; and at the beginning I shall be called mad more than once—until the truth of what I am saying is recognized in all its shattering force."

He wrote to Bismarck asking for an interview in order to submit his plan for a solution to the Jewish problem but he received no reply.

He wrote to Rabbi Gudemann, Chief Rabbi of Vienna, the occasion being the anti-Jewish excesses which had occurred in Vienna. "This plan . . . is a reserve against more evil days."

Herzl, in his first visit to England, met and talked with Israel Zangwill, the novelist, whom he impressed without quite winning him over. But Zangwill made it possible for him to meet more than a few prominent, influential Jews of whom he made immediate converts. None of them wanted to know anything about the Argentine, and on this point the practical men were united with the dreamers: Palestine alone came into the picture for a national concentration of the Jews.

After his experiences in England, Herzl resolved to present his plan to the public at large. The *Address to the Rothschilds* which was the first complete writing of his plan, forged in the heat of inspiration was thoroughly reworked and emerged as his great book *Der Judenstaat.* Its title was: *The Jewish State: An Attempt at a Modern Solution of the Jewish Problem.* Der Judenstaat may properly be called Herzl's life work; his philosophy of the world, his views on the state, on the Jewish people, on science and technology, as we have seen them developing to this, his thirty-fifth year are concentrated in the book.

The "Jewish State" was published in an edition of three thousand. It was read by small circles in various European capitals. It was sent to leading personalities in the press and political circles. It was soon translated into several languages. Herzl received many letters from authors and statesmen in which the work was praised. But the general German press, especially the Jewish-controlled press, took a negative attitude. A number of journalists alluded to the adventurer who would like to become Prime Minister or King of the Jews. No mention of the "Jewish State" appeared in the Neue Freie Presse, then or ever. The Algemeine Zeitung of Vienna said that Zionism was a madness born of despair, The Algemeine Zeitung of Munich described it as a fantastic dream of a feuilletonist whose mind had been unhinged by Jewish enthusiasm.

It was upon the Jewish masses that Herzl made a tremendous impression. He dawned upon Jews of Eastern Europe as a mystic figure rising out of the past. Little was known of his pamphlet, for it was kept out of the country by censorship in Russia. Only its title got their attention

and the stories told of Herzl—the Western Jew returning
to his people—gripped their hearts and stirred their imagination. He was greeted by one of the Galician Zionist
societies as the leader who, like Moses, had returned from
Midian to liberate the Jews. Max Nordau, that devastating
critic of art and literature, was swept off his feet and described the pamphlet as a revelation. Richard Beer Hoffman, the poet, wrote to Herzl saying "At last there comes
again a man, who does not carry his Judaism with resignation as if it were a burden or a misfortune, but is proud
to be the legal heir of an immemorial culture."

It became clear to Herzl that he would have to take an
active part in the task he had set forth in "The Jewish State."
He no longer felt that he stood alone. He was not inclined
to appear on a public platform. He had the shyness of the
man who had always written what he had to say. He also
felt that it would do more harm than good if his ideas were
to be obscured by his personal presence. Through correspondence he set in motion Zionist activities—in London, in
Paris, in Berlin, in the United States. The amount of letter-
writing he developed was enormous.

He decided that there were three tasks to be undertaken
at once. The first was the organization of the Society of
Jews. The second was to continue diplomatic work in Constantinople and among interested Powers. The third was the
creation of a press to influence public opinion and to prepare the Jewish masses for the great migration.

Through the Rev. Hechler, a chaplain of the British Em-
bassy in Vienna, who believed in the Jewish return to the
Holy Land, Herzl was introduced to the Grand Duke of
Baden, a Christian of great piety and influence in political
circles.

Herzl intended to use the influence of the Germans to

affect the Sultan and make him more sympathetic to Zionist proposals. Herzl told the Grand Duke that he would like to have Zionism included within the cultural sphere of German interests. The Grand Duke said that the Kaiser seemed inclined to take Jewish migration under German protection. The great powers were interested in maintaining certain extra territorial rights within the Turkish Empire. If they had nationals in any part of the Empire, they claimed the right to protect them over and above Turkish law. It was, therefore, not the Kaiser's interest in the Jews, but in extending German jurisdiction within the Turkish Empire that persuaded him to suggest the adoption of Jews in Palestine for that purpose. Germany had a special relationship to Turkey. Most of the western powers were openly discussing the impending partition of the Turkish Empire, but Germany was opposed to it.

Herzl was told that the Kaiser was prepared to see him at the head of a delegation when he visited Palestine, but Herzl was anxious to see the Kaiser without delay. He suggested an audience before the trip to Palestine in order that the Kaiser might be in a position to discuss the Jewish question with the Sultan. The Grand Duke advised Herzl to see Count Philip Zu Eulenberg, the German Ambassador at Vienna. Herzl was given an opportunity to see Count Eulenberg in Vienna. Herzl told him that he wanted His Imperial Majesty to persuade the Sultan to open negotiations with the Jews.

The Count passed Herzl over to the German Minister of Foreign Affairs, Von Buelow, who happened to be in Vienna at the same time. Van Buelow knew a great deal about the Zionist movement. He said that the difficulty lay in persuading the Sultan to deal with the Jews. He felt certain that the Sultan could be impressed if he was properly advised by the Kaiser. A week later Herzl was informed of the Kaiser's inclination to take the Jews of Palestine under his protection, and repeated that he would like to see Herzl at the head of a delegation in Jerusalem, later on.

Herzl was afraid of going further in this direction without having in existence the financial instrument without which neither negotiations nor colonization could be carried on. Herzl urged David Wolffsohn and Jacobus Kahn to proceed with the utmost speed to incorporate the Jewish Colonial Trust. He foresaw the possibility that a demand might be made at any time to show the color of his money. Although the affairs of the Bank were in the hands of Wolffsohn and Kahn, Herzl himself worried over every detail, urging and driving and complaining about the slowness of the action. On March 28, 1899 the subscription lists were opened. Herzl's expectations were not fulfilled. Only about 200,000 shares had been sold, three-quarters of them in Russia. The Bank could not be opened until it had at least 250,000 paid-up shares. After a great deal of effort, the minimum was finally obtained and the Trust was officially opened in time for the opening of the third Congress in August, 1899.

Herzl addressed a mass meeting in London in October, 1899, under Dr. Gastner's chairmanship. In his address at this meeting, Herzl said that he believed the time was not far off when the Jewish people would be set in motion. He asked the audience to accept his word even if he could not speak more definitely. "When I return to you again," he said, "we shall, I hope, be still further on our path." At this meeting Father Ignatius, a Catholic believer in Zionism, referred to Herzl "as a new Joshua who had come to fulfill the words of the Prophet Ezekiel." The effect produced upon the audience was not useful to Herzl's purposes at that time. He had always tried to discourage the impression of himself as a Messianic figure. The meeting in London was the only occasion where he lost his self-mastery in public.

When Herzl met the Foreign Minister, Von Buelow, again, it was in the presence of the Reich Chancellor, Hohenlohe. At once he perceived a different nuance in the conversation and a dissonance in comparison with the conversation he had had with Count Eulenberg. He thought that the Chancellor and the Foreign Minister were not in agreement with the Kaiser and did not dare to say it openly; or, on the other hand, they might be favorably inclined but would not be willing to say it to him.

Finally, Herzl saw the Kaiser in Constantinople. After Herzl had introduced the subject of his visit, the Kaiser broke in and explained why the Zionist movement attracted him.

"There are among your people," said the Kaiser, "certain elements whom it would be a good thing to move to Palestine."

He asked Herzl to submit, in advance, the address he intended to present to him in Jerusalem. When he was asked what the Kaiser should place before the Sultan as the gist of the Jewish proposals, Herzl replied "a chartered company under German protection."

Herzl met the Kaiser, as arranged, in Palestine. Herzl arrived in Jaffa on October 6, 1898. On a Friday morning, he awaited the coming of the Kaiser and his entourage on the road that ran by the Colony of Mikveh Israel. The Kaiser recognized him from a distance. He said a few words about the weather, about the lack of water in Palestine, and that it was a land that had a future.

In the petition Herzl later submitted to the Kaiser, many of the pregnant passages were deleted by the Kaiser's ad-

visers. All passages that referred specifically to the aims
of the Zionist movement, to the desperate need of the Jewish people and asking for the Kaiser's protection of a projected Jewish land company for Syria and Palestine, had
been removed. The audience with the Kaiser took place on
Monday, November 2nd. The Kaiser thanked Herzl for
the address which, he said, had interested him extremely.
It was the Kaiser's opinion that the soil was cultivable. What
the land lacked was water and shade.

"That we can supply," said Herzl. "It would cost billions,
but it will bring in billions too."

"Well, you certainly have enough money, more than all
of us," said the Kaiser.

It was a brief interview. It was vague and seemed to lead
nowhere. Herzl was under the impression that certain influences had been exerted between the interview in Constantinople and the audience in Jerusalem.

When the official German communique was issued, the
encounter with Herzl was hid in a closing paragraph and
deprived of all significance. This is how it read:

"Later the Kaiser received the French Consul, also a
Jewish deputation which presented him with an album of
pictures of the Jewish colonies in Palestine. In reply to an
address by the leader of the deputation, His Majesty re-
marked he viewed with benevolent interest all efforts directed
to the improvement of agriculture in Palestine as long as
these accorded with the welfare of the Turkish Empire and
were conducted in a spirit of complete respect for the sovereignty of the Sultan."

It was a sudden descent from hope into a closed road.
Herzl refused to be discouraged. It was hard for him to
realize that the Kaiser's enthusiasm in Constantinople could
have cooled off so quickly in Jerusalem, but it seemed that

there was no way to continue contact with the people he had interested in Germany. He tried to pick up the broken threads, but, once broken, they could not be revived. The Grand Duke of Baden remained ever constant and loyal, but he could do nothing. Herzl never saw the Kaiser again. In a letter to the Grand Duke, closing this chapter of Zionist history, Herzl said:

"I can only assume that a hope especially dear to me has faded away and that we shall not achieve our Zionist goal under a German protectorate."

At about the same time, Herzl met Philip Michael Von Nevlinski, a descendant of a long line of Polish noblemen who had entered the diplomatic service and became a diplomatic agent-at-large and a French journalist. In the first stages, Nevlinski guided Herzl in all the work he did in Constantinople. When Herzl came to Constantinople in June, 1896 he was under the impression that Nevlinski had already arranged an audience with the Sultan. It was not so easy, however. But whether such an audience had been arranged or not, Herzl was able to meet, a number of highly-placed Turkish officials, including the Grand Vizier. At first, the line of action was not clear, but by now Herzl had formulated his proposals to the Sultan.

Ever since the middle of the nineteeth century, Turkish finances had been in a shocking condition. The Empire was being badly managed. The Sultan was regarded as "the sick man of Europe." In 1891 the total external debt, including unpaid interest, reached the figure of two hundred and fifty-three million pounds sterling. In 1881 there was a consolidation of the debt. It was reduced to one hundred and six million pounds, but the finances of Turkey were placed under the control of a committee representing the creditors, to whom was transferred certain domestic Turkish monopolies and the collection of several categories of taxes. This enabled the European powers to intervene in the affairs of Turkey. Only by the removal of this foreign tutelage could Turkey hope to regain its independence. It was to achieve this end, Herzl thought, that the Jews, and the Jews alone, could be useful. For this service, he intended to ask for a Jewish State in Palestine. Herzl followed this line until finally the need for refunding the Turkish debt disappeared.

But at this time Herzl was not able to obtain an audience with the Sultan. Nevlinski reported that such an audience had been refused because the Sultan declined to discuss sovereignty over Palestine. Doubt was expressed as to the accuracy of the report. Whatever the fact may be, the first venture of Herzl in Constantinople was not successful.

Herzl moved along the lines that led to Constantinople and Berlin, but he did not overlook the importance of maintaining contact with Jewish philanthropies. A letter sent to the Baron de Hirsch came a day after his death.

Herzl went to London where matters had been arranged for him to meet the leaders of British Jewry. He met Claude Montefiore and Frederick Mocatte, representatives of the Anglo-Jewish Association. They were not sympathetic. Herzl fared no better at a banquet given to him by the Maccabbeans. The personal impression Herzl made was profound. But there was no practical issue nor did he make any progress during the time he spent in England. He got Sir Samuel Montagu and Colonel Goldsmith to agree to cooperate with him in an endeavor to establish a vassal Jewish State under the sovereignty of Turkey if the Powers would agree; provided, the Baron de Hirsch Fund placed £10,000,-000 at his disposal for the plan; and Baron Edmund de Rothschild became a member of the Executive Committee of the proposed Society of Jews. These conditions were fantastic at that time and Herzl could not meet them.

He went to Paris and had a talk with Baron Edmund. Baron Edmund was older than Herzl and felt ill at ease in the presence of a calm critic of all he had done for Jewish colonization in Palestine. Herzl made the impression on him of an undisciplined enthusiast. Baron Edmund did not believe it possible to create political conditions favorable for a mass immigration of Jews. Even if that could be done, an uncontrolled mass immigration into Palestine would have the effect of landing tens of thousands of Jews to be fed and looked after by the small Jewish community in Palestine. He clung to his idea of slow colonization attracting no attention and careful not to provoke hostility. Every reply of Herzl fell upon a closed mind. Baron Edmund's refusal to co-operate was decisive.

This was a decision of historic significance. It turned Herzl away from the thought that the Zionist movement should be built upon the support of Jewish philanthropy. All his hopes in this connection were dissolved by the contacts he had made in London and in Paris. Baron Edmund's refusal to cooperate carried with it the refusal of the Baron de Hirsch Fund and of the circle of leading Jews in London.

Reluctantly, Herzl came to the conclusion that there was only one reply to this situation. The Jewish masses must be organized for the support of the Zionist movement.

The organization he had in mind was not a popular democratic organization. What he meant was to assemble the upper "cadres" to take charge of the organization of the masses for the great migration. At the same time, he wanted to prove to the philanthropists that a popular organization was possible. He felt that they would be greatly influenced by the development of a widespread popular movement.

Whatever his thoughts were at that time, his decision to turn to the Jewish masses, to abandon reliance upon the wealthy led to the organization of the modern Zionist movement.

He organized his followers in Vienna. He was the center of a circle in which were included the men who later became the members of the first Zionist Actions Committee. In November 1896 he, for the first time, addressed a public meeting in Vienna. In this address he did not use the term "The Jewish State," nor did he use it in most of his public utterances at that time. He had become cautious. He did not want to prejudice his political work in Constantinople.

He was still thinking of issuing a newspaper, but there were no funds for that purpose. The report that he intended to issue a newspaper drew the attention of a number of personalities and groups in Berlin. There were the Russian Jewish students, led by Leo Motzkin, and a group called "Young Israel," headed by Reinrich Loewe. A conference was held on March 6 and 7, 1897, called by Dr. Osias Thon Willy Bambus and Nathan Birnbaum. They had come together to talk about a newspaper but the First Zionist Congress was launched at this meeting Herzl's proposal for the calling of a General Zionist Conference in Munich was agreed to. In the preliminary announcement of the calling of this Conference or Congress, Herzl said:

"The Jewish question must be removed from the control of the benevolent individual. There must be created a forum before which everyone acting for the Jewish people should appear and to which he should be responsible."

Every one of Herzl's ideas was met by protests and public excitement. The protests were usually launched by Jews. The calling of the Congress aroused a great deal of indignation in conservative circles. The Rabbis of Germany protested not only to the holding of the Congress but also the choice of Munich.

The Congress controversy persuaded Herzl to begin the publication of the weekly Die Welt. The first issue appeared on June 4, 1897. Herzl provided the funds. The journal was something new in Jewish life. It was, in fact, the organ of the Congress. Throughout Herzl's life, Die Welt served as the exponent of his ideas. At first, Herzl contributed numerous articles. He sent in a regular weekly review of all activities connected with the movement. He was responsible for many unsigned articles and notices. He directed the paper in all its details, although he refused to figure as its official editor and publisher. The amount of work he did during the months preceding the Congress was amazing. He was completely absorbed in every aspect of the Congress. The man of the pen revealed himself as a first-class man of action.

On August 29, 1897, the First Zionist Congress was assembled, not in Munich but in Basle, Switzerland. The majority of the delegates to the First Zionist Congress, drawn to Basle from all parts of the world, saw Herzl for the first time. The total number of delegates at the first session was 197.

The first act of the Congress was the adoption of a resolution of thanks to the Sultan of Turkey. Then Herzl rose and walked over to the pulpit. It was no longer the elegant Dr. Herzl of Vienna, it was no longer the easy-going literary man, the critic, the feuilletonist. As one reporter said: "It was a scion of the House of David, risen from among the dead, clothed in legend and fantasy and beauty." The first words uttered by Herzl were: "We are here to lay the foundation stone of the house which is to shelter the Jewish nation." "We Zionists," he stressed, "seek for the solution of the Jewish question, not an international society, but an international discussion . . . We have nothing to do with conspiracy, secret intervention or indirect methods. We wish to place the question under the control of free public opinion."

His First Congress address contained the ideas which he had already expressed in previous speeches and articles, but there was a great difference between the views in "The Jewish State" and the address delivered at the first session of the Zionist Congress. The latter is the carefully considered public statement of one who knew he represented tens of thousands, perhaps hundreds of thousands, of followers. His words were not those of a seer, but of a statesman. Almost as profound was the effect produced. It was at this Congress that the Basle Program was adopted . . . "Zionism seeks to secure for the Jewish people a publicly recognized, legally secured home (or homeland) in Palestine."

The second important task of the First Congress was the creation of an organization. The Congress was declared to be "the chief organ of the Zionist movement." The basis of electoral right was to be the payment of a shekel, which at that time was equivalent to twenty-five cents. There was to be an Executive Committee with its permanent seat in Vienna. Everything which was to unfold later in Zionism, both in the way of affirmative forces and inner contradictions, was already visible or latent in the first Congress. There was discussion of a bank, of a land redemption fund to be called The National Fund, the creation of a Hebrew University, and the clashes between practical and political Zionism.

On his return to Vienna, Herzl made the following entry in his diary: "If I were to sum up the Basle Congress in a single phrase I would say: In Basle I created the Jewish

State. Were I to say this aloud I would be greeted by universal laughter. But perhaps five years hence, in any case, certainly fifty years hence, everyone will perceive it. The state exists as essence in the will-to-the-state of a people, yes, even in that will in a single powerful person . . . The territory is only the concrete basis, and the state itself, with a territory beneath it, is still in the nature of an abstract thing . . . In Basle I created the abstraction which, as such, is invisible to the great majority."

All that Herzl did in the political field—his conversations in Constantinople, his interview with the Grand Duke of Baden in advance of the holding of the First Congress, was undertaken as author of a political pamphlet. He was now aware of the fact that he was called upon to act as President of the World Zionist Organization. It was difficult to draw a line between the movement and its leader. Herzl insisted that his leadership in the movement was impersonal and that now its direction was vested in its instruments— the Congress and the Actions Committee. But he had all the authority of an accepted leader.

The evolution of Herzl's conception of the Jewish problem since he saw the degradation of Dreyfus can be measured by a study of the articles he wrote after the First Congress. He himself was quite aware of the transformation. He had seen the Jewish people face to face. "Brothers have found each other again," he said. He wrote with great appreciation of the quality of the Russian delegates. He said, "They possess that inner unity which has disappeared from among the westerners. They are steeped in Jewish national sentiment without betraying any national narrowness and intolerance. They are not tortured by the idea of assimilation. They do not assimilate into other nations, but exert themselves to learn the best in other peoples. In this way they manage to remain erect and genuine. Looking on them, we understood where our forefathers got the strength to endure through the bitterest times."

Immediately after the First Congress, Herzl grappled with his second task, the creation of the Jewish Colonial Bank. He wrote of the bank in *Die Welt* in November, 1898, "The task of the Colonial Bank is to eliminate philanthropy. The settler on the land who increases its value by his labor merits more than a gift. He is entitled to credit. The prospective bank could therefore begin by extending the needed credits to the colonists; later it would expand into the instrument for the bringing in of Jews and would supply credits for transportation, agriculture, commerce and construction."

The seat of the bank was to be London. There were to be two billion shares at £1 each. The bank was to be directed by men acquainted with banking affairs, but the movement would be placed in a position to control its policy. The hopes of Herzl grew from week to week. As he approached the practical situation he became less and less confident of the cooperation of men of wealth. Differences arose in the preliminary discussions as to the scope of the bank. In the first draft of the Articles of Incorporation the Orient alone was named as the area of work for the bank. Menachem Ussishkin insisted that the words "Syria and Palestine" should be substituted. After a great deal of discussion, the proposals for the formation of the bank were brought to the second Zionist Congress and the Articles of Incorporation, as amended, were adopted by acclamation.

Herzl clung to the idea which had come to him when he was thinking of the Jewish State as a pamphlet, that it might be better for him to write a novel. The impulse to write such a novel became irresistible after his visit to Palestine. It was to be called "Altneuland." He began to write it in 1899. It was completed in April 1902, and published six months later. It is remarkable that he could write such a novel while engaged in varied political activities in Constantinople, in London and in Berlin; and while he had to deal with the many troublesome internal Zionist problems.

"Altneuland" was a novel with a purpose. It described the Palestine of the near future as it would develop through the Zionist Movement. It had the weaknesses of every propaganda novel. The entire work has something of the state about it and proceeds in the form of scenes rather than by way of narrative. Each type has a specific outlook. Most of the characters are portraits of living personalities. It was his purpose to memorialize his friends and his opponents.

"Altneuland" tells of a Jew who visits Palestine in 1898 and then comes again in 1923 when he finds the Promised Land developed under Jewish influence. Its territory lies East and West of the Jordan. The dead land of 1898 is now thoroughly alive. Its real creators were the irrigation engineers. Technology had given a new form to labor, a new social and economic system had been created which is described as "mutualistic," a huge cooperative, a mediate form between individualism and collectivism. Haifa had become a world city. Around the Holy City of Jerusalem, modern suburbs had arisen, shaded boulevards and parks, institutes of learning, places of amusement, markets—"a world city in the spirit of the twentieth century." In this new land, the Arabs live side by side in friendship with the Jews.

"Altneuland" did not produce the effect Herzl had expected. Within the Zionist Movement it did more harm than good. Many of Herzl's friends were disappointed that the novel should have so little of the Jewish spirit. It ignored the

Hebraic renaissance. The novel evoked the sharpest criticism from Achad Haam.

* * *

While Herzl was immersed in political action, visiting European capitals, carrying on correspondence with leading persons whose interest in Zionism he had engaged, and submitting reports to the Zionist Congress or to the Actions Committee, often facing critical situations in his struggle with growing Zionist parties, the Zionist Organizaton was gradually becoming an accepted institution in Jewish life. It was the international sounding board for the discussion of the Jewish question. The Jewish National Fund was founded at the Fourth Congress held in London in 1900. The Jewish Colonial Trust was finally established with headquarters in London.

The first Zionist party in the Congress was the Democratic faction led by Leo Motzkin, but soon there were added the Mizrachi party and the beginnings of a labor party. Not only Dr. Nordau's stirring addresses, but many controversies "made" Congresses. The cultural issue was a Congress perennial. Many discussions also took place around what was called the issue of "practical" and "political" Zionism. The Russians, under the leadership of Ussishkin, were all heartily against the "charter" emphasis and drove with maddening persistence for immediate work in Palestine. In the course of these debates, continued over the years, the Congress became a forum for the discussion of international Jewish problems and developed speakers and theorists of varying degrees of talent. It also produced men with hobbies. The Jewish National Fund and the Hebrew University was the hobby of Dr. Herman Schapiro. Colonization in Cyprus was the hobby of Davis Trietsch, who created many scenes on the floor of the Congress. Dr. Chaim Weizmann was not only a leader of the Democratic faction, crossing swords time and again with Herzl, but devoted much time and thought to the idea of a Hebrew University. The procedure of the Congress, based on Continental models, was gradually worked out and became fixed, and many of the delegates were adepts in the art of procedural sparring. The language in Congresses used during Herzl's life was German, but gradually the imperfect use of German by East European Zionists led to the development of what was called "Congress German." This was a form of German that was easy to use, because respect for grammar and pronunciation was not required.

During the Congresses Herzl maintained throughout the role of leader and moderator. His manner was gracious and he never lost his sense of dignity. He was capable of sharp retort, but always bore in mind that it was high duty to hold a balance and to seek compromise rather than sharp division. He developed it in a most remarkable way on the platform. His appearances were dramatic. His interventions were arresting. The man of the writing desk developed as one of the ablest in the parliamentary arts. After some of the Congresses he had to retire to a health resort, having exhausted his strength and bringing on a recurrence of his heart trouble. On a number of occasions his close friends feared for his life. But after a few weeks of rest he usually returned stronger than before and with greater determination to pursue his course, regardless of the consequences to himself.

* * *

At this point it is important to refer to his family life. He had married Julie Naschauer on July 25, 1889. She was the daughter of wealthy parents and grew up in a conventional social circle. When she married Herzl he was already a rising young author who was highly regarded among those with whom she associated. He was attractive, aristocratic in bearing, a keen conversationalist and had all the qualities of being a conventional partner of a conventional wife. But Herzl threw himself into Zionist affairs with such tremendous dynamic activity and was so completely absorbed in the idea which his thinking had given birth to, that except for occasional interim periods, his family played a secondary part in his life ever after he had taken up the Jewish problems his special task in life. Julie Herzl also suffered by reason of Herzl's devotion to his own mother. Herzl never rid himself of his filial dependence which made it very hard for his wife to understand. They had three children. In 1890 a daughter was born and named Paula or Pauline. In 1891 his son, Hans, was born, whose life after his father's death became a serious problem. There was a third child, a daughter Margaret, known as Trude, who was born in May 1893. During this period there were many separations from his family. There were disagreements and reconciliations, but the cup of unhappiness for Julie Herzl overflowed when Herzl became the official leader of a public movement. From that time on her home was constantly overrun with unwelcome visitors. Not only did Herzl give his life to the movement in the literal sense, but he gave his reserve of funds and sacrificed the welfare of his family for the sake of the movement he had brought to life. His domestic affairs as well as his failing heart, made all the years of Herzl's brief Zionist life pain and struggle.

The tragic position of Jews in various parts of Europe, greatly agitated Herzl during the time he was carrying on negotiations with the Kaiser and the Sultan. He was con-

stantly being led to the thought that it would become necessary to find a temporary haven of refuge for Jews. In 1899
a series of pogroms broke out in Galicia. In his diary at the
time, he had references to England and Cyprus, "we may
even have to consider South Africa or America." But he
banished these thoughts from his mind because he knew that
the Zionists would place serious obstacles in the way of con-
sidering any project other than Palestine. When his hopes
with regard to Germany had collapsed, however, he thought
of these alternative proposals again.

* * *

On October 22, 1902 a Conference between Joseph Cham-
berlain, the Colonial Secretary, and Herzl took place.
Chamberlain had been in the Colonial Office since 1895.
He held an influential position in the councils of the British
Government. He was a man of strong will and political inte-
grity. Herzl submitted his plan for the colonization of
Cyprus and the Sinai Peninsula, which included El Arish-
"Jewish settlers under a Jewish administration."

Chamberlain said that he could speak definitely only about
Cyprus. The Sinai Peninsula came under the jurisdiction
of the Foreign Office. As far as Cyprus was concerned, he
believed that it was not promising because the Greeks and
Moslems would object, and it would be his official duty to
side with them. He took a more favorable view, however, of
El Arish. In that connection, it was necessary for Herzl
to talk to Lord Lansdowne of the Foreign Office. A great
deal would depend upon the good-will of Lord Cromer, the
British Consul General in Egypt, and actually the Vice
Regent of that country. Through the good offices of Chamberlain, it became possible for Herzl to meet Lord Lans-

downe a few days later. He was well received and was listened to with a great deal of attention.

Herzl was asked to submit a written expose. Then he asked for permission to have Leopold J. Greenberg go to Egypt and confer with Lord Cromer. Lord Lansdowne said that he would arrange for such a meeting. Greenberg discussed the matter with Lord Cromer in Cairo. There were objections raised by both Lord Cromer and the Egyptian Prime Minister on the ground that an attempted Jewish economy, undertaken in 1891-2 in the region of ancient Midian, had been a pitiful failure. There had been political complications and border disputes with Turkey.

A definitive reply was received by Herzl on December 18, 1902 written on behalf of Lord Lansdowne by Sir T. H. Sanderson, permanent Undersecretary. Lord Lansdowne had heard from Lord Cromer, who favored the sending of a small commission to the Sinai Peninsula to report on conditions and prospects, but Lord Cromer feared that no sanguine hopes of success should be entertained, but if the report of the Commission turned out favorable, the Egyptian Government would certainly offer liberal terms for Jewish colonization.

On the other hand, however, the Zionists should understand that they would be expected to meet the cost of a defense corps and to guarantee the administration. In Lord Cromer's opinion, the most important question was that of the rights which Herzl expected for the projected settlement. He wrote: "In your letter of the 12th ult. you remark that you will become great and promising by the granting of this right of colonization. Your letter does not make clear what is to be understood by these words, and what kind of rights the colonists will expect."

Lord Lansdowne also touched on the question of the new

citizenship of the settlers. Herzl had believed that he would have only Englishmen to deal with, since England had become more and more the master of Egypt. It was apparent, however, that the Egyptian Government also played an important part in the discussions.

Lord Cromer confirmed that the Egyptian Government would make it an essential condition that the new settlers become Turkish subjects bound by Egyptian law, but while the British occupation continued the settlers would always be certain of fair treatment.

Herzl was satisfied with this letter and described it as a historic document. The British Government had recognized Herzl as the Zionist leader, and the movement represented by him as a negotiating party. He already saw the "Egyptian province of Judea" under a Jewish Governor, with its own defense corps under Anglo-Egyptian officers.

As a result of the English negotiations, Lord Rothschild seemed to be won over by Herzl. The old banker, who had refused two years before to meet the Zionist leader, now visited him in his hotel. The next task before Herzl was the organization of the Commission. The Commission was composed of the South African engineer, Kessler; the Chief Inspector of the Egyptian Survey Department, Humphreys; Col. Goldsmith was to report on the land; and Dr. Soskin was to study agricultural possibilities. Oscar Marmorek was to investigate building and housing problems and act as General Secretary. Dr. Hillel Jaffe of the Jaffe Hospital was to deal with the problems of climate and hygiene.

The Commission met with great difficulties. There was opposition by the Turks. There was misunderstandings between Herzl and Greenberg. Herzl himself went to Egypt in order to bring the negotiations to a conclusion and to straighten out difficulties. His intervention in no way im-

proved the situation. Lord Cromer had become very cool
toward him. He received the general report of the Commission, which observed that "under existing conditions the
land is quite unsuitable for settlers from European countries, but if sufficient irrigation were introduced, the agricultural, hygienic and climatic conditions are such that part
of the land, which is at present wilderness, could support
a considerable population."

An application for the concession was made by Herzl on
the advice of Lord Cromer, having as his legal representative
a Belgian lawyer of high standing. The Egyptian Government did not receive with favor the outline of the concession.
Herzl was received on April 23rd by Chamberlain, who had
just returned from his African journey. Chamberlain listened
to the report given by Herzl on the work of the Commission. Both regarded the report as unfavorable. Then Chamberlain made this remark:

"On my travels I saw a country for you, Uganda. On the
coast it is hot, but in the interior the climate is excellent
for Europeans. You can plant cotton and sugar. I thought
to myself, that is just the country for Dr. Herzl. But *he*
must have Palestine, and will move only into its vicinity."

This was the first reference to Uganda which became the
center of attention in Zionist circles.

Herzl was told that the Egyptian Government would reject
the plan. It was found that the area would require five times
as much water as had been first estimated. The Egyptian
Government could not permit the diversion of such a quantity of water from the Nile.

An attempt to have Chamberlain intervene with Egypt was
not successful. "That being the case," said Chamberlain,
"What about Uganda?" Self-administration would be accorded. The Governor could definitely be a Jew. Although

the matter belonged to the Foreign Office, he would have it transferred under his jurisdiction in the colonial office. The territory would be the permanent property of a colonization company created for the purpose. After five years, the settlers would be given complete autonomy. The name of the settlement was to be "New Palestine."

Herzl pressed for a reply from the government in order that the project might be presented to the Zionist Congress on August 14, 1903. The official proposal came from Sir Clement Hill, permanent head of the Foreign Office. In this letter it was stated that Lord Landsdowne had studied the question with the interest which His Majesty's Government always felt bound to take in every serious plan destined to better the condition of the Jewish race. The time had been too short for a closer examination of the plan and for its submission to the British representative for the East African (Uganda) Protectorate. "Lord Landsdowne assumes," the letter continues, "that the Bank desires to send a number of gentlemen to the East African Protectorate to establish whether there is in that territory land suitable for the purpose in view; should this prove to be the case, he will be happy to give them every assistance in bringing them together with His Majesty's Congress, the conditions under which the settlement could be carried out. Should an area be found which the bank and His Majesty's representative consider suitable, and His Majesty's government consider desirable, Lord Lansdowne will be glad to consider favorably proposals for the creation of a Jewish colony or settlement under such conditions as will seem to the members to guarantee the retention of their national customs . . . "

The document went on with an offer—subject to the consent of the relevant officials—of a Jewish governorship and internal autonomy.

This was the first official proposal in connection with the
Zionist movement which Herzl was able to submit to a
Zionist Congress. When the letter of Sir Clement Hill was
submitted to the Sixth Zionist Congress in 1903, it split
the Zionist movement wide open. It arrayed the overwhelming majority of Zionists in Russia against Herzl and
he was called upon to defend himself against a general
attack which preceded the convening of the Congress. When
the Congress was convened in an atmosphere of great excitement and partisan controversy, the Uganda project was
submitted in the form of an official resolution calling for
the appointment of a commission of nine to be sent to investigate conditions in East Africa. The final decision on the
report of the investigating committee was to be left to a
special Congress. Although the vote showed a majority in
favor of the official resolution—the tally was 295 for, 177
against, and 100 absentees—the debate on the resolution
revealed an overwhelming opposition to the project. It was
regarded as an abandonment of Palestine in favor of a
diversion. After the vote, the Russian delegates left the
Congress in a body. All the opposition delegates left with
them and met in conference to discuss the situation. When
Herzl heard of the deep feeling that prevailed in the conference, he asked for the privilege of speaking to the opposition. He gave them his solemn assurance that the Basle
Program would be unaffected by the resolution. He swore
fealty to the Basle Program, to Zion and Jerusalem. His
speech revealed the great transformation that had taken
place in Herzl's organic relation to the Zionist movement.
The opposition delegates felt that in spite of Herzl's seeking alternately one or another substitute for Palestine, his
heart responded without reserve to the appeal of Zion. The
opposition reappeared in the Congress the following day.

They exacted assurances that the funds of the Jewish Colonial Trust, of the Jewish National Fund and the Shekel Income, should not be used for the commission investigating East Africa, and that the commission should report to the Greater Actions Committee before it appeared to submit its report to the Congress.

Herzl's experience at what is called the "Uganda Congress" drew him nearer to the older Zionists. He realized now that the ultimate goal could not be reached within the near future, that Uganda was merely a compromise achievement, providing the field of preparation for a second attempt to reach Zion. The Congress of 1903 was the climax of Herzl's career. It was, in effect, the end of his quest.

Later, the East African project became a matter of lesser importance in the eyes of the English. The English colonists in East Africa declared their opposition to a Jewish settlement. A Zionist opposition was organized, led by Menahem Ussishkin, who was not present at the Uganda Congress. The Charkov Conference of Russian Zionists was called. Herzl was charged with having violated the Basle Program. The Charkov Conference disclaimed responsibility for all actions in the direction of East Africa. It appointed a committee of three to communicate their demands to Herzl. They asked that he promise that he would not place before the Congress any territorial projects other than those connected with Palestine or Syria, and that he would take East Africa off the agenda. By now Herzl would have been pleased to let the East African project disappear from the agenda; it was clear that the English government was not greatly interested and was seeking a way out; but the devious route of political action, once started, could not so easily be halted; Herzl found himself chained to a political reality.

Throughout his Zionist life, Herzl suffered from a heart

ailment which became more and more acute as he was taken up by the excitements and activities of the Movement. He became aware of his illness soon after he had written "The Jewish State." He had premonitions of the fatal consequences but persisted in carrying the burden of the Movement himself, consuming all his strength in the process. At intervals he was forced to take rest cures. On a number of occasions it was thought that he had reached the end of his strength. When he was grappling with the Uganda project, York-Steiner, an intimate friend, wrote of his appearance: "The imposing figure is now stooped, the face sallow, the eyes—the mirrors of a fine soul—were darkened, the mouth was drawn in pain and marked by passion."

He was almost at the brink of the grave. In May, an alarming change for the worse occurred in the condition of his heart muscles. He was ordered to Franzienbad for six weeks, but the rest did him no good. On June 3, he left with his wife and several friends for Edlach in Semmering. He knew that this was his last journey. Then there was a slight improvement and he returned to his desk. But he rapidly grew worse. To the faithful Hechler he said, "Give them all my greetings and tell them that I have given my heart's blood for my people." On July 3, pneumonia set in and there were signs of approaching exhaustion. His mother arrived, then his two younger children, Hans and Trude. At five in the afternoon, his physician who had taken his eyes off the patient for a moment, heard a deep sigh. When he turned, he saw Herzl's head sunk on his breast.

In his will Herzl asked that his body be buried next to his father, "to remain there until the Jewish people will carry my remains to Palestine." When the Russians entered Vienna in 1945 the remains of Herzl were still there.

The Jewish State

by

Theodor Herzl

Preface

THE IDEA WHICH I HAVE DEVELOPED IN THIS PAMPHLET is a very old one: it is the restoration of the Jewish State.

The world resounds with outcries against the Jews, and these outcries have awakened the slumbering idea.

I wish it to be clearly understood from the outset that no portion of my argument is based on a new discovery. I have discovered neither the historic condition of the Jews nor the means to improve it. In fact, every man will see for himself that the materials of the structure I am designing are not only in existence, but actually already in hand. If, therefore, this attempt to solve the Jewish Question is to be designated by a single word, let it be said to be the result of an inescapable conclusion rather than that of a flighty imagination.

I must, in the first place, guard my scheme from being treated as Utopian by superficial critics who might commit this error of judgment if I did not warn them. I should obviously have done nothing to be ashamed of if I had described a Utopia on philanthropic lines; and I should also, in all probability, have obtained literary success more easily if I had set forth my plan in the irresponsible guise of a romantic tale. But this Utopia is far less attractive than any one of those portrayed by Sir Thomas More and his numerous forerunners and successors. And I believe that the situation of the Jews in many countries is grave enough to make such preliminary trifling superfluous.

An interesting book, "Freiland," by Dr. Theodor Hertzka, which appeared a few years ago, may serve to mark the distinction I draw between my conception and a Utopia. His is the ingenious invention of a modern mind thoroughly schooled in the principles of political economy, it is as remote from actuality as the Equatorial mountain on which his dream State lies. "Freiland" is a complicated piece of mechanism with numerous cogged wheels fitting into each other; but there is nothing to prove that they can be set in motion. Even supposing "Freiland societies" were to come into existence, I should look on the whole thing as a joke.

The present scheme, on the other hand, includes the employment of an existent propelling force. In consideration of my own inadequacy, I shall content myself with indicating the cogs and wheels of the machine to be constructed, and I shall rely on more skilled mechanicians than myself to put them together.

Everything depends on our propelling force. And what is that force? The misery of the Jews.

Who would venture to deny its existence? We shall discuss it fully in the chapter on the causes of Anti-Semitism.

Everybody is familiar with the phenomenon of steam-power, generated by boiling water, which lifts the kettle-lid. Such tea-kettle phenomena are the attempts of Zionist and kindred associations to check Anti-Semitism.

I believe that this power, if rightly employed, is powerful enough to propel a large engine and to move passengers and goods: the engine having whatever form men may choose to give it.

I am absolutely convinced that I am right, though I doubt whether I shall live to see myself proved to be so. Those who are the first to inaugurate this movement will scarcely live to see its glorious close. But the inauguration of it is enough to give them a feeling of pride and the joy of spiritual freedom.

I shall not be lavish in artistically elaborated descriptions of my project, for fear of incurring the suspicion of painting a Utopia. I anticipate, in any case, that thoughtless scoffers will caricature my sketch and thus try to weaken its effect. A Jew, intelligent in other respects, to whom I explained my plan, was of the opinion that "a Utopia was a project whose future details were represented as already extant." This is a fallacy. Every Chancellor of the Exchequer calculates in his Budget estimates with assumed figures, and not only with such as are based on the average returns of past years, or on previous revenues in other States, but sometimes with figures for which there is no precedent whatever; as for example, in instituting a new tax. Everybody who studies a Budget knows that this is the case. But even if it were known that the estimates would not be rigidly adhered to, would such a financial draft be considered Utopian?

But I am expecting more of my readers. I ask the cultivated men whom I am addressing to set many preconceived ideas entirely aside. I shall even go so far as to ask those Jews who have most earnestly tried to solve the Jewish Question to look upon their previous attempts as mistaken and futile.

I must guard against a danger in setting forth my idea. If I describe future circumstances with too much caution I shall appear to doubt their possibility. If, on the other hand, I announce their realization with too much assurance I shall appear to be describing a chimera.

I shall therefore clearly and emphatically state that I believe in the practical outcome of my scheme, though without professing to have discovered the shape it may ultimately take. The Jewish State is essential to the world; it will therefore be created.

The plan would, of course, seem absurd if a single individual attempted to do it; but if worked by a number of Jews in co-operation it would appear perfectly rational, and its accomplishment would present no difficulties worth mentioning. The idea depends only on the number of its supporters. Perhaps our ambitious young men, to whom every road of progress is now closed, seeing in this Jewish State a bright prospect of freedom, happiness and honors opening to them, will ensure the propagation of the idea.

I feel that with the publication of this pamphlet my task is done. I shall not again take up the pen, unless the attacks of noteworthy antagonists drive me to do so, or it becomes necessary to meet unforeseen objections and to remove errors.

Am I stating what is not yet the case? Am I before my time? Are the sufferings of the Jews not yet grave enough? We shall see.

It depends on the Jews themselves whether this political pamphlet remains for the present a political romance. If the present generation is too dull to understand it rightly, a future, finer and a better generation will arise to understand it. The Jews who wish for a State shall have it, and they will deserve to have it.

Chapter I.—Introduction

IT IS ASTONISHING HOW LITTLE INSIGHT INTO THE science of economics many of the men who move in the midst of active life possess. Hence it is that even Jews faithfully repeat the cry of the Anti-Semites: "We depend for sustenance on the nations who are our hosts, and if we had no hosts to support us we should die of starvation." This is a point that shows how unjust accusations may weaken our self-knowledge. But what are the true grounds for this statement concerning the nations that act as "hosts"? Where it is not based on limited physiocratic views it is founded on the childish error that commodities pass from hand to hand in continuous rotation. We need not wake from long slumber, like Rip van Winkle, to realize that the world is considerably altered by the production of new commodities. The technical progress made during this wonderful era enables even a man of most limited intelligence to note with his short-sighted eyes the appearance of new commodities all around him. The spirit of enterprise has created them.

Labor without enterprise is the stationary labor of ancient days; and typical of it is the work of the husbandman, who stands now just where his progenitors stood a thousand years ago. All our material welfare has been brought about by men of enterprise. I feel almost ashamed of writing down so trite a remark. Even if we were a nation of entrepreneurs—such as absurdly exaggerted accounts make us out to be—we should not require another nation to live on. We do not depend on the circulation of old commodities, because we produce new ones.

The world possesses slaves of extraordinary capacity for work, whose appearance has been fatal to the production of handmade goods: these slaves are the machines. It is true that workmen are required to set machinery in motion; but for this we have men in plenty, in super-abundance. Only those who are ignorant of the conditions of Jews in many countries of Eastern Europe would venture to assert that Jews are either unfit or unwilling to perform manual labor.

But I do not wish to take up the cudgels for the Jews in this pamphlet. It would be useless. Everything rational and everything sentimental that can possibly be said in their defence has been said already. If one's hearers are incapable of comprehending them, one is a preacher in a desert. And if one's hearers are broad and high-minded enough to have grasped them already, then the sermon is superfluous. I believe in the ascent of man to higher and yet higher grades of civilization; but I consider this ascent to be desperately slow. Were we to wait till average humanity had become as charitably inclined as was Lessing when he wrote "Nathan the Wise," we should wait beyond our day, beyond the days of our children, of our grandchildren, and of our great-grandchildren. But the world's spirit comes to our aid in another way.

This century has given the world a wonderful renaissance by means of its technical achievements; but at the same time its miraculous improvements have not been employed in the service of humanity. Distance has ceased to be an obstacle, yet we complain of insufficient space. Our great steamships carry us swiftly and surely over hitherto unvisited seas. Our railways carry us safely into a mountain-world hitherto tremblingly scaled on foot. Events occurring in countries undiscovered when Europe confined the Jews in Ghettos are known to us in the course of an hour. Hence the misery of the Jews is an anachronism—not because there was a period of enlightenment one hundred years ago, for that enlightenment reached in reality only the choicest spirits.

I believe that electric light was not invented for the purpose of illuminating the drawing-rooms of a few snobs, but rather for the purpose of throwing light on some of the dark problems of humanity. One of these problems, and not the least of them, is the Jewish question. In solving it we are working not only for ourselves, but also for many other over-burdened and oppressed beings.

The Jewish question still exists. It would be foolish to deny it. It is a remnant of the Middle Ages, which civilized nations do not even yet seem able to shake off, try as they will. They certainly showed a generous desire to do so when they emancipated us. The Jewish question exists wherever Jews live in perceptible numbers. Where it does not exist, it is carried by Jews in the course of their migrations. We naturally move to those places where we are not persecuted, and there our presence produces persecution. This is the case in every country, and will remain so, even in those highly civilized—for instance, France—until the Jewish question finds a solution on a political basis. The unfortunate Jews are now carrying the seeds of Anti-Semitism into England; they have already introduced it into America.

I believe that I understand Anti-Semitism, which is really a highly complex movement. I consider it from a Jewish standpoint, yet without fear or hatred. I believe that I can see what elements there are in it of vulgar sport, of common trade jealousy, of inherited prejudice, of religious intolerance, and also of pretended self-defence. I think the Jewish

question is no more a social than a religious one, notwith-
standing that it sometimes takes these and other forms.
It is a national question, which can only be solved by
making it a political world-question to be discussed and
settled by the civilized nations of the world in council.

the Jewish question

We are a people—one people.

We have honestly endeavored everywhere to merge ourselves in the social life of surrounding communities and to
preserve the faith of our fathers. We are not permitted to do so. In vain are we loyal patriots, our loyalty
in some places running to extremes; in vain do we make
the same sacrifices of life and property as our fellow-
citizens; in vain do we strive to increase the fame of our
native land in science and art, or her wealth by trade and
commerce. In countries where we have lived for centuries
we are still cried down as strangers, and often by those
whose ancestors were not yet domiciled in the land where
Jews had already had experience of suffering. The majority may decide which are the strangers; for this, as indeed every point which arises in the relations between
nations, is a question of might. I do not here surrender
any portion of our prescriptive right, when I make this
statement merely in my own name as an individual. In
the world as it now is and for an indefinite period will
probably remain, might precedes right. It is useless, therefore, for us to be loyal patriots, as were the Huguenots
who were forced to emigrate. If we could only be left in
peace. . . .

But I think we shall not be left in peace.

Oppression and persecution cannot exterminate us. No
nation on earth has survived such struggles and sufferings
as we have gone through. Jew-baiting has merely stripped
off our weaklings; the strong among us were invariably

true to their race when persecution broke out against them. This attitude was most clearly apparent in the period immediately following the emancipation of the Jews. Those Jews who were advanced intellectually and materially entirely lost the feeling of belonging to their race. Wherever our political well-being has lasted for any length of time, we have assimilated with our surroundings. I think this is not discreditable. Hence, the statesman who would wish to see a Jewish strain in his nation would have to provide for the duration of our political well-being; and even a Bismarck could not do that.

For old prejudices against us still lie deep in the hearts of the people. He who would have proofs of this need only listen to the people where they speak with frankness and simplicity: proverb and fairy-tale are both Anti-Semitic. A nation is everywhere a great child, which can certainly be educated; but its education would, even in most favorable circumstances, occupy such a vast amount of time that we could, as already mentioned, remove our own difficulties by other means long before the process was accomplished.

[handwritten margin note: end of Anti-Sem through educ. would take too long to b a viable option]

Assimilation, by which I understood not only external conformity in dress, habits, customs, and language, but also identity of feeling and manner—assimilation of Jews could be effected only by intermarriage. But the need for mixed marriages would have to be felt by the majority; their mere recognition by law would certainly not suffice.

The Hungarian Liberals, who have just given legal sanction to mixed marriages, have made a remarkable mistake which one of the earliest cases clearly illustrates; a baptized Jew married a Jewess. At the same time the struggle to obtain the present form of marriage accentuated distinctions between Jews and Christians, thus hindering rather than aiding the fusion of races.

Those who really wished to see the Jews disappear through intermixture with other nations, can only hope to see it come about in one way. The Jews must previously acquire economic power sufficiently great to overcome the old social prejudice against them. The aristocracy may serve as an example of this, for in its ranks occur the proportionately largest numbers of mixed marriages. The Jewish families which regild the old nobility with their money become gradually absorbed. But what form would this phenomenon assume in the middle classes, where (the Jews being a bourgeois people) the Jewish question is mainly concentrated? A previous acquisition of power could be synonymous with that economic supremacy which Jews are already erroneously declared to possess. And if the power they now possess creates rage and indignation among the Anti-Semites, what outbreaks would such an increase of power create? Hence the first step towards absorption will never be taken, because this step would involve the subjection of the majority to a hitherto scorned minority, possessing neither military nor administrative power of its own. I think, therefore, that the absorption of Jews by means of their prosperity is unlikely to occur. In countries which now are Anti-Semitic my view will be approved. In others, where Jews now feel comfortable, it will probably be violently disputed by them. My happier co-religionists will not believe me till Jew-baiting teaches them the truth; for the longer Anti-Semitism lies in abeyance the more fiercely will it break out. The infiltration of immigrating Jews, attracted to a land by apparent security, and the ascent in the social scale of native Jews, combine powerfully to bring about a revolution. Nothing is plainer than this rational conclusion.

assimilation, esp. via intermarriage. not the answer

Because I have drawn this conclusion with complete indifference to everything but the quest of truth, I shall probably be contradicted and opposed by Jews who are in easy circumstances. Insofar as private interests alone are held by their anxious or timid possessors to be in danger, they can safely be ignored, for the concerns of the poor and oppressed are of greater importance than theirs. But I wish from the outset to prevent any misconception from arising, particularly the mistaken notion that my project, if realized, would in the least degree injure property now held by Jews. I shall therefore explain everything connected with rights of property very fully. Whereas, if my plan never becomes anything more than a piece of literature, things will merely remain as they are. It might more reasonably be objected that I am giving a handle to Anti-Semitism when I say we are a people—one people; that I am hindering the assimilation of Jews where it is about to be consummated, and endangering it where it is an accomplished fact, insofar as it is possible for a solitary writer to hinder or endanger anything.

This objection will be especially brought forward in France. It will probably also be made in other countries, but I shall answer only the French Jews beforehand, because these afford the most striking example of my point.

However much I may worship personality—powerful individual personality in statesmen, inventors, artists, philosophers, or leaders, as well as the collective personality of a historic group of human beings, which we call a nation—however much I may worship personality, I do not regret its disappearance. Whoever can, will, and must perish, let him perish. But the distinctive nationality of Jews neither can, will, nor must be destroyed. It cannot be destroyed, because external enemies consolidate it. It

Anti-Semitism helped to create + reinforces Jewish nationalism

will not be destroyed; this is shown during two thousand years of appalling suffering. It must not be destroyed, and that, as a descendant of numberless Jews who refused to despair, I am trying once more to prove in this pamphlet. Whole branches of Judaism may wither and fall, but the trunk will remain.

Hence, if all or any of the French Jews protest against this scheme on account of their own "assimilation," my answer is simple: The whole thing does not concern them at all. They are Jewish Frenchmen, well and good! This is a private affair for the Jews alone.

The movement towards the organization of the State I am proposing would, of course, harm Jewish Frenchmen no more than it would harm the "assimilated" of other countries. It would, on the contrary, be distinctly to their advantage. For they would no longer be disturbed in their "chromatic function," as Darwin puts it, but would be able to assimilate in peace, because the present Anti-Semitism would have been stopped for ever. They would certainly be credited with being assimilated to the very depths of their souls, if they stayed where they were after the new Jewish State, with its superior institutions, had become a reality.

The "assimilated" would profit even more than Christian citizens by the departure of faithful Jews; for they would be rid of the disquieting, incalculable, and unavoidable rivalry of a Jewish proletariat, driven by poverty and political pressure from place to place, from land to land. This floating proletariat would become stationary. Many Christian citizens—whom we call Anti-Semites—can now offer determined resistance to the immigration of foreign Jews. Jewish citizens cannot do this, although it affects them far more directly; for on them they feel first of all the keen competition of individuals carrying on similar branches of industry, who, in addition, either introduce Anti-Semitism where it does not exist, or intensify it where it does. The "assimilated" give expression to this secret grievance in "philanthropic" undertakings. They organize emigration societies for wandering Jews. There is a reverse to the picture which would be comic, if it did not deal with human beings. For some of these charitable institutions are created not for, but against, persecuted Jews; they are created to despatch these poor creatures just as fast and far as possible. And thus, many an apparent friend of the Jews turns out, on careful inspection, to be nothing more than an Anti-Semite of Jewish origin, disguised as a philanthropist.

But the attempts at colonization made even by really benevolent men, interesting attempts though they were, have so far been unsuccessful. I do not think that this or that man took up the matter merely as an amusement, that they engaged in the emigration of poor Jews as one indulges in the racing of horses. The matter was too grave and tragic for such treatment. These attempts were interesting, in that they represented on a small scale the practical fore-runners of the idea of a Jewish State. They were even useful, for out of their mistakes may be gathered experience for carrying the idea out successfully on a larger scale. They have, of course, done harm also. The transportation of Anti-Semitism to new districts, which is the inevitable consequence of such artificial infiltration, seems to me to be the least of these evils. Far worse is the circumstance that unsatisfactory results tend to cast doubts on intelligent men. What is impractical or impossible to simple argument will remove this doubt from the minds of intelligent men. What is unpractical or impossible to

lg. scale migration will/can succeed where limited/sm scale emigration fails

accomplish on a small scale, need not necessarily be so on a larger one. A small enterprise may result in loss under the same conditions which would make a large one pay. A rivulet cannot even be navigated by boats, the river into which it flows carries stately iron vessels.

No human being is wealthy or powerful enough to transplant a nation from one habitation to another. An idea alone can achieve that and this idea of a State may have the requisite power to do so. The Jews have dreamt this kingly dream all through the long nights of their history. "Next year in Jerusalem" is our old phrase. It is now a question of showing that the dream can be converted into a living reality.

For this, many old, outgrown, confused and limited notions must first be entirely erased from the minds of men. Dull brains might, for instance, imagine that this exodus would be from civilized regions into the desert. That is not the case. It will be carried out in the midst of civilization. We shall not revert to a lower stage, we shall rise to a higher one. We shall not dwell in mud huts; we shall build new more beautiful and more modern houses, and possess them in safety. We shall not lose our acquired possessions; we shall realize them. We shall surrender our well earned rights only for better ones. We shall not sacrifice our beloved customs; we shall find them again. We shall not leave our old home before the new one is prepared for us. Those only will depart who are sure thereby to improve their position; those who are now desperate will go first, after them the poor; next the prosperous, and, last of all, the wealthy. Those who go in advance will raise themselves to a higher grade, equal to those whose representatives will shortly follow. Thus the exodus will be at the same time an ascent of the class.

Is this marxist?

The departure of the Jews will involve no economic disturbances, no crises, no persecutions; in fact, the countries they abandon will revive to a new period of prosperity. There will be an inner migration of Christian citizens into the positions evacuated by Jews. The outgoing current will be gradual, without any disturbance, and its initial movement will put an end to Anti-Semitism. The Jews will leave as honored friends, and if some of them return, they will receive the same favorable welcome and treatment at the hands of civilized nations as is accorded to all foreign visitors. Their exodus will have no resemblance to a flight, for it will be a well-regulated movement under control of public opinion. The movement will not only be inaugurated with absolute conformity to law, but it cannot even be carried out without the friendly cooperation of interested Governments, who would derive considerable benefits from it.

Security for the integrity of the idea and the vigor of its execution will be found in the creation of a body corporate, or corporation. This corporation will be called "The Society of Jews." In addition to it there will be a Jewish company, an economically productive body.

An individual who attempted even to undertake this huge task alone would be either an impostor or a madman. The personal character of the members of the corporation will guarantee its integrity, and the adequate capital of the Company will prove its stability.

These prefatory remarks are merely intended as a hasty reply to the mass of objections which the very words "Jewish State" are certain to arouse. Henceforth we shall proceed more slowly to meet further objections and to explain in detail what has been as yet only indicated; and we shall try in the interests of this pamphlet to avoid making it a dull exposition. Short aphoristic chapters will therefore best answer the purpose.

If I wish to substitute a new building for an old one, I must demolish before I construct. I shall therefore keep to this natural sequence. In the first and general part 1 shall explain my ideas, remove all prejudices, determine essential political and economic conditions, and develop the plan.

In the special part, which is divided into three principal sections, I shall describe its execution. These three sections are: The Jewish Company, Local Groups, and the Society of Jews. The Society is to be created first, the Company last; but in this exposition the reverse order is preferable, because it is the financial soundness of the enterprise which will chiefly be called into question, and doubts on this score must be removed first.

In the conclusion, I shall try to meet every further objection that could possibly be made. My Jewish readers will, I hope, follow me patiently to the end. Some will naturally make their objections in an order of succession other than that chosen for their refutation. But whoever finds his doubts dispelled should give allegiance to the cause.

Although I speak of reason, I am fully aware that reason alone will not suffice. Old prisoners do not willingly leave their cells. We shall see whether the youth whom we need are at our command—the youth, who irresistibly draw on the old, carry them forward on strong arms, and transform rational motives into enthusiasm.

II.—The Jewish Question

No ONE CAN DENY THE GRAVITY OF THE SITUATION OF the Jews. Wherever they live in perceptible numbers, they are more or less persecuted. Their equality before the law, granted by statute, has become practically a dead letter. They are debarred from filling even moderately high positions, either in the army, or in any public or private capacity. And attempts are made to thrust them out of business also: "Don't buy from Jews!"

Attacks in Parliaments, in assemblies, in the press, in the pulpit, in the street, on journeys—for example, their exclusion from certain hotels—even in places of recreation, become daily more numerous. The forms of persecutions varying according to the countries and social circles in which they occur. In Russia, imposts are levied on Jewish villages; in Rumania, a few persons are put to death; in Germany, they get a good beating occasionally; in Austria, Anti-Semites exercise terrorism over all public life; in Algeria, there are travelling agitators; in Paris, the Jews are shut out of the so-called best social circles and excluded from clubs. Shades of anti-Jewish feeling are innumerable. But this is not to be an attempt to make out a doleful category of Jewish hardships.

I do not intend to arouse sympathetic emotions on our behalf. That would be foolish, futile, and undignified proceeding. I shall content myself with putting the following questions to the Jews: Is it not true that, in countries where we live in perceptible numbers, the position of Jewish lawyers, doctors, technicians, teachers, and employees of all descriptions becomes daily more intolerable? Is it not true,

85

that the Jewish middle classes are seriously threatened? Is it not true, that the passions of the mob are incited against our wealthy people? Is it not true, that our poor endure greater sufferings than any other proletariat? I think that this external pressure makes itself felt everywhere. In our economically upper classes it causes discomfort, in our middle classes continual and grave anxieties, in our lower classes absolute despair.

Everything tends, in fact, to one and the same conclusion, which is clearly enunciated in that classic Berlin phrase: *"Juden Raus!"* (Out with the Jews!)

I shall now put the Question in the briefest possible form: Are we to "get out" now and where to?

Or, may we yet remain? And, how long?

Let us first settle the point of staying where we are. Can we hope for better days, can we possess our souls in patience, can we wait in pious resignation till the princes and peoples of this earth are more mercifully disposed towards us? I say that we cannot hope for a change in the current of feeling. And why not? Even if we were as near to the hearts of princes as are their other subjects, they could not protect us. They would only feel popular hatred by showing us too much favor. By "too much," I really mean less than is claimed as a right by every ordinary citizen, or by every race. The nations in whose midst Jews live are all either covertly or openly Anti-Semitic.

The common people have not, and indeed cannot have, any historic comprehension. They do not know that the sins of the Middle Ages are now being visited on the nations of Europe. We are what the Ghetto made us. We have attained pre-eminence in finance, because mediae-val conditions drove us to it. The same process is now being repeated. We are again being forced into finance, now it is the stock exchange, by being kept out of other branches of economic activity. Being on the stock exchange, we are consequently exposed afresh to contempt. At the same time we continue to produce an abundance of mediocre intellects who find no outlet, and this endangers our social position as much as does our increasing wealth. Educated Jews without means are now rapidly becoming Socialists. Hence we are certain to suffer very severely in the struggle between classes, because we stand in the most exposed position in the camps of both Socialists and capitalists.

PREVIOUS ATTEMPTS AT A SOLUTION

The artificial means heretofore employed to overcome the troubles of Jews have been either too petty—such as attempts at colonization—or attempts to convert the Jews into peasants in their present homes.

What is achieved by transporting a few thousand Jews to another country? Either they come to grief at once, or prosper, and then their prosperity creates Anti-Semitism. We have already discussed these attempts to divert poor Jews to fresh districts. This diversion is clearly inadequate and futile, if it does not actually defeat its own ends; for it merely protracts and postpones a solution, and perhaps even aggravates difficulties.

Whoever would attempt to convert the Jew into a husbandman would be making an extraordinary mistake. For a peasant is in a historical category, as proved by his costume which in some countries he has worn for centuries; and by his tools, which are identical with those used by his earliest forefathers. His plough is unchanged; he carries the seed in his apron; mows with the historical scythe, and threshes with the time-honored flail. But we know that all this can be done by machinery. The agrarian question is only a question of machinery. America must conquer Europe, in the same way as large landed possessions absorb small ones. The peasant is consequently a type which is in course of extinction. Whenever he is artificially preserved, it is done on account of the political interests which he is intended to serve. It is absurd, and indeed impossible, to make modern peasants on the old pattern. No one is wealthy or powerful enough to make civilization take a single retrograde step. The mere preservation of obsolete institutions is a task severe enough to require the enforcement of all the despotic measures of an autocratically governed State.

Are we, therefore, to credit Jews who are intelligent with a desire to become peasants of the old type? One might just as well say to them: "Here is a cross-bow: now go to war!" What? With a cross-bow, while the others have rifles and long range guns? Under these circumstances the Jews are perfectly justified in refusing to stir when people try to make peasants of them. A cross-bow is a beautiful weapon, which inspires me with mournful feelings when I have time to devote to them. But it belongs by rights to a museum.

Now, there certainly are districts to which desperate Jews go out, or at any rate, are willing to go out and till the soil. And a little observation shows that these districts—such as the enclave of Hesse in Germany, and some provinces in Russia—these very districts are the principal seats of Anti-Semitism.

For the world's reformers, who send the Jews to the plough, forget a very important person, who has a great deal to say on the matter. This person is the agriculturist, and the agriculturist is also perfectly justified. For the tax on land, the risks attached to crops, the pressure of large proprietors who cheapen labor, and American competition in particular, combine to make his life hard enough. Besides, the duties on corn cannot go on increasing indefinitely. Nor can the manufacturer be allowed to starve; his political influence is, in fact, in the ascendant, and he must therefore be treated with additional consideration.

All these difficulties are well known, therefore I refer to them only cursorily. I merely wanted to indicate clearly how futile had been past attempts—most of them well intentioned—to solve the Jewish Question. Neither a diversion of the stream, nor an artificial depression of the intellectual level of our proletariat, will overcome the difficulty. The supposed infallible expedient of assimilation has already been dealt with.

We cannot get the better of Anti-Semitism by any of these methods. It cannot die out so long as its causes are not removed. Are they removable?

CAUSES OF ANTI-SEMITISM

We shall not again touch on those causes which are a result of temperament, prejudice and narrow views, but shall here restrict ourselves to political and economical causes alone. Modern Anti-Semitism is not to be confounded with the religious persecution of the Jews of former times. It does occasionally take a religious bias in some countries, but the main current of the aggressive movement has now changed. In the principal countries where Anti-Semitism prevails, it does so as a result of the emancipation of the Jews. When civilized nations awoke to the inhumanity of discriminatory legislation and en-

franchised us, our enfranchisement came too late. It was
no longer possible to remove our disabilities in our old
homes. For we had, curiously enough, developed while
in the Ghetto into a bourgeois people, and we stepped out
of it only to enter into fierce competition with the middle
classes. Hence, our emancipation set us suddenly within
this middle-class circle, where we have a double pressure
to sustain, from within and from without. The Christian
bourgeoisie would not be unwilling to cast us as a sacrifice
to Socialism, though that would not greatly improve matters.

At the same time, the equal rights of Jews before the
law cannot be withdrawn where they have once been conceded. Not only because their withdrawal would be opposed to the spirit of our age, but also because it would
immediately drive all Jews, rich and poor alike, into the
ranks of subversive parties. Nothing effectual can really
be done to our injury. In olden days our jewels were
seized. How is our movable property to be got hold of
now? It consists of printed papers which are locked
up somewhere or other in the world, perhaps in the coffers
of Christians. It is, of course, possible to get at shares
and debentures in railways, banks and industrial undertakings of all descriptions by taxation, and where the
progressive income-tax is in force all our movable property
can eventually be laid hold of. But all these efforts cannot
be directed against Jews alone, and wherever they might
nevertheless be made, severe economic crises would be their
immediate consequences, which would be by no means
confined to the Jews who would be the first affected. The
very impossibility of getting at the Jews nourishes and
embitters hatred of them. Anti-Semitism increases day by
day and hour by hour among the nations; indeed, it is
bound to increase, because the causes of its growth con-

tinue to exist and cannot be removed. Its remote cause is our loss of the power of assimilation during the Middle Ages; its immediate cause is our excessive production of mediocre intellects, who cannot find an outlet downwards or upwards—that is to say, no wholesome outlet in either direction. When we sink, we become a revolutionary proletariat, the subordinate officers of all revolutionary parties; and at the same time, when we rise, there rises also our terrible power of the purse.

EFFECTS OF ANTI-SEMITISM

The oppression we endure does not improve us, for we are not a whit better than ordinary people. It is true that we do not love our enemies; but he alone who can conquer himself dare reproach us with that fault. Oppression naturally creates hostility against oppressors, and our hostility aggravates the pressure. It is impossible to escape from this eternal circle.

"No!" Some soft-hearted visionaries will say: "No, it is possible! Possible by means of the ultimate perfection of humanity."

Is it necessary to point to the sentimental folly of this view? He who would found his hope for improved conditions on the ultimate perfection of humanity would indeed be relying upon a Utopia!

I referred previously to our "assimilation". I do not for a moment wish to imply that I desire such an end. Our national character is too historically famous, and, in spite of every degradation, too fine to make its annihilation desirable. We might perhaps be able to merge ourselves entirely into surrounding races, if these were to leave us in peace for a period of two generations. But they will not leave us in peace. For a little period they manage to tolerate us, and then their hostility breaks out again and again. The world is provoked somehow by our prosperity, because it has for many centuries been accustomed to consider us as the most contemptible among the poverty-stricken. In its ignorance and narrowness of heart, it fails to observe that prosperity weakens our Judaism and extinguishes our peculiarities. It is only pressure that forces us back to the parent stem; it is only hatred encompassing us that makes us strangers once more.

Thus, whether we like it or not, we are now, and shall henceforth remain, a historic group with unmistakable characteristics common to us all.

We are one people—our enemies have made us one without our consent, as repeatedly happens in history. Distress binds us together, and, thus united, we suddenly discover our strength. Yes, we are strong enough to form a State, and, indeed, a model State. We possess all human and material resources necessary for the purpose.

This is therefore the appropriate place to give an account of what has been somewhat roughly termed our "human material." But it would not be appreciated till the broad lines of the plan, on which everything depends, has first been marked out.

THE PLAN

The whole plan is in its essence perfectly simple, as it must necessarily be if it is to come within the comprehension of all.

Let the sovereignty be granted us over a portion of the globe large enough to satisfy the rightful requirements of a nation; the rest we shall manage for ourselves.

The creation of a new State is neither ridiculous nor

impossible. We have in our day witnessed the process in connection with nations which were not largely members of the middle class, but poorer, less educated, and consequently weaker than ourselves. The Governments of all countries scourged by Anti-Semitism will be keenly interested in assisting us to obtain the sovereignty we want.

The plan, simple in design, but complicated in execution, will be carried out by two agencies: The Society of Jews and the Jewish Company.

The Society of Jews will do the preparatory work in the domains of science and politics, which the Jewish Company will afterwards apply practically.

The Jewish Company will be the liquidating agent of the business interests of departing Jews, and will organize commerce and trade in the new country.

We must not imagine the departure of the Jews to be a sudden one. It will be gradual, continuous, and will cover many decades. The poorest will go first to cultivate the soil. In accordance with a preconceived plan, they will construct roads, bridges, railways and telegraph installations; regulate rivers; and build their own dwellings; their labor will create trade, trade will create markets and markets will attract new settlers, for every man will go voluntarily, at his own expense and his own risk. The labor expended on the land will enhance its value, and the Jews will soon perceive that a new and permanent sphere of operation is opening here for that spirit of enterprise which has heretofore met only with hatred and obloquy.

If we wish to found a State today, we shall not do it in the way which would have been the only possible one a thousand years ago. It is foolish to revert to old stages of civilization, as many Zionists would like to do. Supposing, for example, we were obliged to clear a country of wild beasts, we should not set about the task in the fashion of Europeans of the fifth century. We should not take spear and lance and go out singly in pursuit of bears; we would organize a large and active hunting party, drive the animals together, and throw a melinite bomb into their midst.

If we wish to conduct building operations, we shall not plant a mass of stakes and piles on the shore of a lake, but we shall build as men build now. Indeed, we shall build in a bolder and more stately style than was ever adopted before, for we now possess means which men never yet possessed.

The emigrants standing lowest in the economic scale will be slowly followed by those of a higher grade. Those who at this moment are living in despair will go first. They will be led by the mediocre intellects which we produce so superabundantly and which are persecuted everywhere.

This pamphlet will open a general discussion on the Jewish Question, but that does not mean that there will be any voting on it. Such a result would ruin the cause from the outset, and dissidents must remember that allegiance or opposition is entirely voluntary. He who will not come with us should remain behind.

Let all who are willing to join us, fall in behind our banner and fight for our cause with voice and pen and deed.

Those Jews who agree with our idea of a State will attach themselves to the Society, which will thereby be authorized to confer and treat with Governments in the name of our people. The Society will thus be acknowledged in its relations with Governments as a State-creating power. This acknowledgment will practically create the State.

Should the Powers declare themselves willing to admit our sovereignty over a neutral piece of land, then the Society will enter into negotiations for the possession of this land. Here two territories come under consideration, Palestine and Argentine. In both countries important experiments in colonization have been made, though on the mistaken principle of a gradual infiltration of Jews. An infiltration is bound to end badly. It continues till the inevitable moment when the native population feels itself threatened, and forces the Government to stop a further influx of Jews. Immigration is consequently futile unless we have the sovereign right to continue such immigration.

The Society of Jews will treat with the present masters of the land, putting itself under the protectorate of the European Powers, if they prove friendly to the plan. We could offer the present possessors of the land enormous advantages, assume part of the public debt, build new roads for traffic, which our presence in the country would render necessary, and do many other things. The creation of our State would be beneficial to adjacent countries, because the cultivation of a strip of land increases the value of its surrounding districts in innumerable ways.

PALESTINE OR ARGENTINE?

Shall we choose Palestine or Argentine? We shall take what is given us, and what is selected by Jewish public opinion. The Society will determine both these points.

Argentine is one of the most fertile countries in the world, extends over a vast area, has a sparse population and a mild climate. The Argentine Republic would derive considerable profit from the cession of a portion of its territory to us. The present infiltration of Jews has cer-

tainly produced some discontent, and it would be necessary to enlighten the Republic on the intrinsic difference
of our new movement.

Palestine is our ever-memorable historic home. The very
name of Palestine would attract our people with a force
of marvellous potency. If His Majesty the Sultan were
to give us Palestine, we could in return undertake to
regulate the whole finances of Turkey. We should there
form a portion of a rampart of Europe against Asia, an
outpost of civilization as opposed to barbarism. We should
as a neutral State remain in contact with all Europe, which
would have to guarantee our existence. The sanctuaries
of Christendom would be safeguarded by assigning to
them an extra-territorial status such as is well-known to
the law of nations. We should form a guard of honor about
these sanctuaries, answering for the fulfilment of this duty
with our existence. This guard of honor would be the great
symbol of the solution of the Jewish Question after eighteen
centuries of Jewish suffering.

DEMAND, MEDIUM, TRADE

I said in the last chapter, "The Jewish Company will
organize trade and commerce in the new country." I shall
here insert a few remarks on that point.

A scheme such as mine is gravely imperilled if it is opposed by "practical" people. Now "practical" people are
as a rule nothing more than men sunk into the groove of
daily routine, unable to emerge from a narrow circle of
antiquated ideas. At the same time, their adverse opinion
carries great weight, and can do considerable harm to a
new project, at any rate until this new thing is sufficiently
strong to throw the "practical" people and their mouldy
notions to the winds.

In the earliest period of European railway construction some "practical" people were of the opinion that it was foolish to build certain lines "because there were not even sufficient passengers to fill the mail-coaches." They did not realize the truth—which now seems obvious to us—that travellers do not produce railways, but, conversely, railways produce travellers, the latent demand, of course, is taken for granted.

The impossibility of comprehending how trade and commerce are to be created in a new country which has yet to be acquired and cultivated, may be classed with those doubts of "practical" persons concerning the need of railways. A "practical" person would express himself somewhat in this fashion:

"Granted that the present situation of the Jews is in many places unendurable, and aggravated day by day; granted that there exists a desire to emigrate; granted even that the Jews do emigrate to the new country; how will they earn their living there, and what will they earn? What are they to live on when there? The business of many people cannot be artificially organized in a day."

To this I should reply: We have not the slightest intention of organizing trade artificially, and we should certainly not attempt to do it in a day. But, though the organization of it may be impossible, the promotion of it is not. And how is commerce to be encouraged? Through the medium of a demand. The demand recognized, the medium created, it will establish itself.

If there is a real earnest demand among Jews for an improvement of their status; if the medium to be created—the Jewish Company—is sufficiently powerful, then commerce will extend itself freely in the new country.

III. The Jewish Company
OUTLINES

THE JEWISH COMPANY IS PARTLY MODELLED ON THE lines of a great land-acquisition company. It might be called a Jewish Chartered Company, though it cannot exercise sovereign power, and has other than purely colonial tasks.

The Jewish Company will be founded as a joint stock company subject to English jurisdiction, framed according to English laws, and under the protection of England. Its principal center will be London. I cannot tell yet how large the Company's capital should be; I shall leave that calculation to our numerous financiers. But to avoid ambiguity, I shall put it at a thousand million marks (about £50,000,000 or $200,000,000); it may be either more or less than that sum. The form of subscription, which will be further elucidated, will determine what fraction of the whole amount must be paid in at once.

The Jewish Company is an organization with a transitional character. It is strictly a business undertaking, and must be carefully distinguished from the Society of Jews.

The Jewish Company will first of all convert into cash all vested interests left by departing Jews. The method adopted will prevent the occurrences of crises, secure every man's property, and facilitate that inner migration of Christian citizens which has already been indicated.

NON-TRANSFERABLE GOODS

The non-transferable goods which come under consideration are buildings, land, and local business connections.

The Jewish Company will at first take upon itself no more than the necessary negotiations for effecting the sale of these goods. These Jewish sales will take place freely and without any serious fall in prices. The Company's branch establishments in various towns will become the central offices for the sale of Jewish estates, and will charge only so much commission on transactions as will ensure their financial stability.

The development of this movement may cause a considerable fall in the prices of landed property, and may eventually make it impossible to find a market for it. At this juncture the Company will enter upon another branch of its functions. It will take over the management of abandoned estates till such time as it can dispose of them to the greatest advantage. It will collect house rents, let out land on lease, and install business managers—these, on account of the required supervision, being, if possible, tenants also. The Company will endeavor everywhere to facilitate the acquisition of land by its tenants, who are Christians. It will, indeed, gradually replace its own officials in the European branches by Christian substitutes (lawyers, etc.); and these are not by any means to become servants of the Jews; they are intended to be free agents to the Christian population, so that everything may be carried through in equity, fairness and justice, and without imperilling the internal welfare of the people.

At the same time the Company will sell estates, or, rather, exchange them. For a house it will offer a house in the new country; and for land, land in the new country; everything being, if possible, transferred to the new soil in the same state as it was in the old. And this transfer will be a great and recognized source of profit to the Company. "Over there" the houses offered in exchange will be newer, more beautiful, and more comfortably fitted, and the landed estates of greater value than those abandoned; but they will cost the Company comparatively little, because it will have bought the ground very cheaply.

PURCHASE OF LAND

The land which the Society of Jews will have secured by international law must, of course, be privately acquired.

Provisions made by individuals for their own settlement do not come within the province of this general account. But the Company will require large areas for its own needs and ours, and these it must secure by centralized purchase. It will negotiate principally for the acquisition of fiscal domains, with the great object of taking possession of this land "over there" without paying a price too high, in the same way as it sells here without accepting one too low. A forcing of prices is not to be considered, because the value of the land will be created by the Company through its organizing the settlement in conjunction with the supervising Society of Jews. The latter will see to it that the enterprise does not become a Panama, but a Suez.

The Company will sell building sites at reasonable rates to its officials, and will allow them to mortgage these for the building of their homes, deducting the amount due from their salaries, or putting it down to their account as increased emolument. This will, in addition to the honors they expect, will be additional pay for their services.

All the immense profits of this speculation in land will go to the Company, which is bound to receive this indefinite premium in return for having borne the risk of the undertaking. When the undertaking involves any risk, the profits must be freely given to those who have borne it. But under no other circumstances will profits be permitted. Financial morality consists in the correlation of risk and profit.

BUILDINGS

The Company will thus barter houses and estates. It must be plain to any one who has observed the rise in the value of land through its cultivation that the Company will be bound to gain on its landed property. This can best be seen in the case of enclosed pieces of land in town and country. Areas not built over increase in value through surrounding cultivation. The men who carried out the extension of Paris made a successful speculation in land which was ingenious in its simplicity; instead of erecting new buildings in the immediate vicinity of the last houses of the town, they bought up adjacent pieces of land, and began to build on the outskirts of these. This inverse order of construction raised the value of building sites with extraordinary rapidity, and, after having completed the outer ring, they built in the middle of the town on these highly valuable sites, instead of continually erecting houses at the extremity.

Will the Company do its own building, or employ independent architects? It can, and will, do both. It has, as will be shown shortly, an immense reserve of working power, which will not be sweated by the Company, but, transported into brighter and happier conditions of life, will nevertheless not be expensive. Our geologists will have looked to the provision of building materials when they selected the sites of the towns.

What is to be the principle of construction?

WORKMEN'S DWELLINGS

The workmen's dwellings (which include the dwellings

of all operatives) will be erected at the Company's own risk and expense. They will resemble neither those melancholy workmen's barracks of European towns, nor those miserable rows of shanties which surround factories; they will certainly present a uniform appearance, because the Company must build cheaply where it provides the building materials to a great extent; but the detached houses in little gardens will be united into attractive groups in each locality. The natural conformation of the land will rouse the ingenuity of our young architects, whose ideas have not yet been cramped by routine; and even if the people do not grasp the whole import of the plan, they will at any rate feel at ease in their loose clusters. The Temple will be visible from long distances, for it is only our ancient faith that has kept us together. There will be light, attractive, healthy schools for children, conducted on the most approved modern systems. There will be continuation-schools for workmen, which will educate them in greater technical knowledge and enable them to become intimate with the working of machinery. There will be places of amusement for the proper conduct of which the Society of Jews will be responsible.

We are, however, speaking merely of the buildings at present, and not of what may take place inside of them.

I said that the Company would build workmen's dwellings cheaply. And cheaply, not only because of the proximity of abundant building materials, not only because of the Company's proprietorship of the sites, but also because of the non-payment of workmen.

American farmers work on the system of mutual assistance in the construction of houses. This childishly amicable system, which is as clumsy as the block-houses erected, can be developed on much finer lines.

totally planned communities

UNSKILLED LABORERS

Our unskilled laborers, who will come at first from the great reservoirs of Russia and Rumania, must, of course, render each other assistance, in the construction of houses. They will be obliged to build with wood in the beginning, because iron will not be immediately available. Later on the original, inadequate, makeshift buildings will be replaced by superior dwellings.

Our unskilled laborers will first mutually erect these shelters; and then they will earn their houses as permanent possessions by means of their work—not immediately, but after three years of good conduct. In this way we shall secure energetic and able men, and these men will be practically trained for life by three years of labor under good discipline.

I said before that the Company would not have to pay these unskilled laborers. What will they live on?

On the whole, I am opposed to the Truck system,* but it will have to be applied in the case of these first settlers. The Company provides for them in so many ways, that it may take charge of their maintenance. In any case the Truck system will be enforced only during the first few years, and it will benefit the workmen by preventing their being exploited by small traders, landlords, etc. The Company will thus make it impossible from the outset for those of our people, who are perforce hawkers and peddlers here, to reestablish themselves in the same trades over there. And the Company will also keep back drunkards and dissolute men. Then will there be no payment of wages at all during the first period of settlement. Certainly, there will be wages for overtime.

---

* The practice of paying the workman's wages in goods instead of money.

THE SEVEN-HOUR DAY

The seven-hour day is the regular working day.

This does not imply that wood-cutting, digging, stone-breaking, and a hundred other daily tasks should only be performed during seven hours. Indeed not. There will be fourteen hours of labor, work being done in shifts of three and a half hours. The organization of all this will be military in character; there will be commands, promotions and pensions, the means by which these pensions are provided being explained further on.

A sound man can do a great deal of concentrated work in three and a half hours. After an interval of the same length of time—which he will devote to rest, to his family, and to his education under guidance—he will be quite fresh for work again. Such labor can do wonders.

The seven-hour day thus implies fourteen hours of joint labor—more than that cannot be put into a day.

I am convinced that it is quite possible to introduce this seven-hour day with success. The attempts to do so in Belgium and England are well known. Some advanced political economists who have studied the subject, declare that a five-hour day would suffice. The Society of Jews and the Jewish Company will, in any case, make new and extensive experiments which will benefit the other nations of the world; and if the seven-hour day proves itself practicable, it will be introduced in our future State as the legal and regular working day.

Meantime, the Company will always allow its employees the seven-hour day; and it will always be in a position to do so.

The seven-hour day will be the call to summon our people in every part of the world. All must come voluntarily, for ours must indeed be the Promised Land. . . .

Whoever works longer than seven hours receives his additional pay for overtime in cash. Seeing that all his needs are supplied, and that those members of his family who are unable to work are provided for by transplanted and centralized philanthropic institutions, he can save a little money. Thrift, which is already a characteristic of our people, should be greatly encouraged, because it will, in the first place, facilitate the rise of individuals to higher grades; and secondly, the money saved will provide an immense reserve fund for future loans. Overtime will only be permitted on a doctor's certificate, and must not exceed three hours. For our men will crowd to work in the new country, and the world will see then what an industrious people we are.

I shall not describe the mode of carrying out the Truck system, nor, in fact, the innumerable details of any process, for fear of confusing my readers. Women will not be allowed to perform any arduous labor, nor to work overtime.

Pregnant women will be relieved of all work, and will be supplied with nourishing food by the Truck. We want our future generations to be strong men and women.

We shall educate children as we wish from the commencement; but this I shall not elaborate either.

My remarks on workmen's dwellings, and on unskilled laborers and their mode of life, are no more Utopian than the rest of my scheme. Everything I have spoken of is already being put into practice, only on an utterly small scale, neither noticed nor understood. The "Assistance par le Travail," which I learned to know and understand in Paris, was of great service to me in the solution of the Jewish question.

RELIEF BY LABOR

The system of relief by labor which is now applied in
Paris, in many other French towns, in England, in Switzerland, and in America, is a very small thing, but capable
of the greatest expansion.

What is the principle of relief by labor?

The principle is: to furnish every needy man with easy,
unskilled work, such as chopping wood, or cutting faggots
used for lighting stoves in Paris households. This is a
kind of prison-work before the crime, done without loss of
character. It is meant to prevent men from taking to crime
out of want, by providing them with work and testing
their willingness to do it. Starvation must never be allowed
to drive men to suicide; for such suicides are the deepest
disgrace to a civilization which allows rich men to throw
tid-bits to their dogs.

Relief by labor thus provides every one with work. But
the system has a great defect; there is not a sufficiently
large demand for the production of the unskilled workers
employed, hence there is a loss to those who employ them;
though it is true that the organization is philanthropic,
and therefore prepared for loss. But here the benefaction
lies only in the difference between the price paid for the
work and its actual value. Instead of giving the beggar
two sous, the institution supplies him with work on which
it loses two sous. But at the same time it converts the good-
for-nothing beggar into an honest breadwinner, who has
earned perhaps 1 franc 50 centimes. 150 centimes for 10!
That is to say, the receiver of a benefaction in which there
is nothing humiliating has increased it fifteenfold! That
is to say, fifteen thousand millions for one thousand millions!

The institution certainly loses 10 centimes. But the Jewish
Company will not lose one thousand millions; it will draw

enormous profits from this expenditure.

There is a moral side also. The small system of relief by labor which exists now preserves rectitude through industry till such time as the man who is out of work finds a post suitable to his capacities, either in his old calling or in a new one. He is allowed a few hours daily for the purpose of looking for a place, in which task the institutions assist him.

The defect of these small organizations, so far, has been that they have been prohibited from entering into competition with timber merchants, etc. Timber merchants are electors; they would protest, and would be justified in protesting. Competition with State prison-labor has also been forbidden, for the State must occupy and feed its criminals.

In fact, there is very little room in an old-established society for the successful application of the system of "Assistance par le Travail."

But there is room in a new society.

For, above all, we require enormous numbers of unskilled laborers to do the first rough work of settlement, to lay down roads, plant trees, level the ground, construct railroads, telegraph installations, etc. All this will be carried out in accordance with a large and previously settled plan.

COMMERCE

The labor carried to the new country will naturally create trade. The first markets will supply only the absolute necessities of life; cattle, grain, working clothes, tools, arms—to mention just a few things. These we shall be obliged at first to procure from neighboring States, or from Europe; but we shall make ourselves independent as soon as possible. The Jewish entrepreneurs will soon realize the business prospects that the new country offers.

The army of the Company's officials will gradually introduce more refined requirements of life. (Officials include officers of our defensive forces, who will always form about a tenth part of our male colonists. They will be sufficiently numerous to quell mutinies, for the majority of our colonists will be peaceably inclined.)

The refined requirements of life introduced by our officials in good positions will create a correspondingly improved market, which will continue to better itself. The married man will send for wife and children, and the single for parents and relatives, as soon as a new home is established "over there." The Jews who emigrate to the United States always proceed in this fashion. As soon as one of them has daily bread and a roof over his head, he sends for his people; for family ties are strong among us. The Society of Jews and the Jewish Company will unite in caring for and strengthening the family still more, not only morally, but materially also. The officials will receive additional pay on marriage and on the birth of children, for we need all who are there, and all who will follow.

OTHER CLASSES OF DWELLINGS

I described before only workmen's dwellings built by themselves, and omitted all mention of other classes of dwellings. These I shall now touch upon. The Company's architects will build for the poorer classes of citizens also, being paid in kind or cash; about a hundred different types of houses will be erected, and, of course, repeated. These beautiful types will form part of our propaganda. The soundness of their construction will be guaranteed by the Company, which will, indeed, gain nothing by selling them to settlers at a fixed sum. And where will these houses be situated? That will be shown in the section dealing with Local Groups.

Seeing that the Company does not wish to earn anything on the building works but only on the land, it will desire as many architects as possible to build by private contract. This system will increase the value of landed property, and it will introduce luxury, which serves many purposes. Luxury encourages arts and industries, paving the way to a future subdivision of large properties.

Rich Jews who are now obliged carefully to secrete their valuables, and to hold their dreary banquets behind lowered curtains, will be able to enjoy their possessions in peace, "over there." If they cooperate in carrying out this emigration scheme, their capital will be rehabilitated and will have served to promote an unexampled undertaking. If in the new settlement rich Jews begin to rebuild their mansions which are stared at in Europe with such envious eyes, it will soon become fashionable to live over there in beautiful modern houses.

SOME FORMS OF LIQUIDATION

The Jewish Company is intended to be the receiver and administrator of the non-transferable goods of the Jews.

Its methods of procedure can be easily imagined in the case of houses and estates, but what methods will it adopt in the transfer of businesses?

Here numberless processes may be found practicable, which cannot all be enlarged on in this outline. But none of them will present any great difficulties, for in each case the business proprietor, when he voluntarily decides to emigrate, will settle with the Company's officers in his district on the most advantageous form of liquidation.

This will most easily be arranged in the case of small employers, in whose trades the personal activity of the proprietor is of chief importance, while goods and organization are a secondary consideration. The Company will provide a certain field of operation for the emigrant's personal activity, and will substitute a piece of ground, with loan of machinery, for his goods. Jews are known to adapt themselves with remarkable ease to any form of earning a livelihood, and they will quickly learn to carry on a new industry. In this way a number of small traders will become small landholders. The Company will, in fact, be prepared to sustain what appears to be a loss in taking over the non-transferable property of the poorest emigrants; for it will thereby induce the free cultivation of tracts of land, which raises the value of adjacent tracts.

In medium-sized businesses, where goods and organization equal, or even exceed, in importance, the personal activity of the manager, whose larger connection is also non-transferable, various forms of liquidation are possible. Here comes an opportunity for that inner migration of Christian citizens into positions evacuated by Jews. The departing Jew will not lose his personal business credit, but will carry it with him, and make good use of it in a new country to establish himself. The Jewish Company will open a current bank account for him. And he can sell the goodwill of his original business, or hand it over to the control of managers under supervision of the Company's officials. The managers may rent the business or buy it, paying for it by instalments. But the Company acts temporarily as curator for the emigrants, in superintending, through its officers and lawyers, the administration of their affairs, and seeing to the proper collection of all payments.

If a Jew cannot sell his business, or entrust it to a proxy or wish to give up its personal management, he may stay where he is. The Jews who stay will be none the worse off, for they will be relieved of the competition of those who leave, and will no longer hear the Anti-Semitic cry: "Don't buy from Jews!"

If the emigrating business proprietor wishes to carry on his old business in the new country, he can make his arrangements for it from the very commencement. An example will best illustrate my meaning. The firm X carries on a large business in dry goods. The head of the firm wishes to emigrate. He begins by setting up a branch establishment in his future place of residence, and sending out samples of his stock. The first poor settlers will be his first customers; these will be followed by emigrants of a higher class, who require superior goods. X then sends out newer goods, and eventually ships his newest. The branch establishment begins to pay while the principal one is still in existence, so that X ends by having two paying business-houses. He sells his original business or hands it over to his Christian representative to manage, and goes off to take charge of the new one.

Another and greater example: Y and Son are large coal-traders, with mines and factories of their own. How is so huge and complex a property to be liquidated? The mines and everything connected with them might, in the first place, be bought up by the State, in which they are situated. In the second place, the Jewish Company might take them over, paying for them partly in land, partly in cash. A third method might be the conversion of "Y and Son" into a limited company. A fourth method might be the continued working of the business under the original proprietors, who would return at intervals to inspect their property, as foreigners, and as such, under the protection of law in every civilized State. All these suggestions are carried out daily. A fifth and excellent method, and one which might be particularly profitable, I shall merely indicate, because the existing examples of its working are at present few, however ready the modern consciousness may be to adopt them. Y and Son might sell their enterprise to the collective body of their employees, who would form a cooperative society, with limited liability, and might perhaps pay the requisite sum with the help of the State Treasury, which does not charge high interest.

The employees would then gradually pay off the loan, which either the Government or the Jewish Company, or even Y and Son, would have advanced to them.

The Jewish Company will be prepared to conduct the transfer of the smallest affairs equally with the largest. And whilst the Jews quietly emigrate and establish their new homes, the Company acts as the great controlling body, which organizes the departure, takes charge of deserted possessions, guarantees the proper conduct of the movement with its own visible and tangible property, and provides permanent security for those who have already settled.

SECURITIES OF THE COMPANY

What assurance will the Company offer that the abandonment of countries will not cause their impoverishment and produce economic crises?

I have already mentioned that honest Anti-Semites, whilst preserving their independence, will combine with our officials in controlling the transfer of our estates.

But the State revenues might suffer by the loss of a body of taxpayers, who, though little appreciated as citizens, are highly valued in finance. The State should, therefore, receive compensation for this loss. This we offer indirectly by leaving in the country businesses which we have built up by means of Jewish acumen and Jewish industry, by letting our Christian fellow-citizens move into our evacuated positions, and by this facilitating the rise of numbers of people to greater prosperity so peaceably and in so unparalleled a manner. The French Revolution had a somewhat similar result, on a small scale, but it was brought about by bloodshed on the guillotine in every province of France, and on the battlefields of Europe. Moreover, inherited and acquired rights were destroyed, and only cunning buyers enriched themselves by the purchase of State properties.

The Jewish Company will offer to the States that come within its sphere of activity direct as well as indirect advantages. It will give Governments the first offer of abandoned Jewish property, and allow buyers most favorable conditions. Governments, again, will be able to make use of this friendly appropriation of land for the purpose of certain social improvements.

The Jewish Company will give every assistance to Governments and Parliaments in their efforts to direct the inner migration of Christian citizens.

The Jewish Company will also pay heavy taxes. Its central office will be in London, so as to be under the legal protection of a power which is not at present Anti-Semitic. But the Company, if it is supported officially and semi-officially, will everywhere provide a broad basis of taxation. To this end, it will establish taxable branch offices everywhere. Further, it will pay double duties on the two-fold transfer of goods which it accomplishes. Even in transactions where the Company is really nothing more than

a real estate agency, it will temporarily appear as a pur-
chaser, and will be set down as the momentary possessor
in the register of landed property.

These are, of course, purely calculable matters. It will
have to be considered and decided in each place how far
the Company can go without running any risks of failure.
And the Company itself will confer freely with Finance
Ministers on the various points at issue. Ministers will
recognize the friendly spirit of our enterprise, and will consequently offer every facility in their power necessary for
the successful achievement of the great undertaking.

Further and direct profit will accrue to Governments
from the transport of passengers and goods, and where
railways are State property the returns will be immediately recognizable. Where they are held by private com-
panies, the Jewish Company will receive favorable terms
for transport, in the same way as does every transmitter
of goods on a large scale. Freight and carriage must be
made as cheap as possible for our people, because every
traveller will pay his own expenses. The middle classes
will travel with Cook's tickets, the poorer classes in emigrant trains. The Company might make a good deal by
reductions on passengers and goods; but here, as elsewhere, it must adhere to its principle of not trying to raise
its receipts to a greater sum than will cover its working
expenses.

In many places Jews have control of the transport; and
the transport businesses will be the first needed by the
Company and the first to be liquidated by it. The original
owners of these concerns will either enter the Company's
service, or establish themselves independently "over there."
The new arrivals will certainly require their assistance,
and theirs being a paying profession, which they may and

indeed must exercise there to earn a living, numbers of these enterprising spirits will depart. It is unnecessary to describe all the business details of this monster expedition. They must be judiciously evolved out of the original plan by many able men, who must apply their minds to achieving the best system.

SOME OF THE COMPANY'S ACTIVITIES

Many activities will be interconnected. For example: the Company will gradually introduce the manufacture of goods into the settlements which will, of course, be extremely primitive at their inception. Clothing, linens, and shoes will first of all be manufactured for our own poor emigrants, who will be provided with new suits of clothing at the various European emigration centers. They will not receive these clothes as alms, which might hurt their pride, but in exchange for old garments: any loss the Company sustains by this transaction will be booked as a business loss. Those who are absolutely without means will pay off their debt to the Company by working overtime at a fair rate of wage.

Existing emigration societies will be able to give valuable assistance here, for they will do for the Company's colonists what they did before for departing Jews. The forms of such cooperation will easily be found.

Even the new clothing of the poor settlers will have the symbolic meaning. "You are now entering on a new life." The Society of Jews will see to it that long before the departure and also during the journey a serious yet festive spirit is fostered by means of prayers, popular lectures, instruction on the object of the expedition, instruction on hygienic matters for their new places of residence, and guidance in regard to their future work. For the

communist "cultural indoctrination"?

Promised Land is the land of work. On their arrival, the
emigrants will be welcomed by our chief officials with due
solemnity, but without foolish exultation, for the Promised
Land will not yet have been conquered. But these poor
people should already see that they are at home.

The clothing industries of the Company will, of course,
not produce their goods without proper organization. The
Society of Jews will obtain from the local branches information about the number, requirements and date of arrival of the settlers, and will communicate all such information in good time to the Jewish Company. In this way
it will be possible to provide for them with every precaution.

PROMOTION OF INDUSTRIES

The duties of the Jewish Company and the Society of
Jews cannot be kept strictly apart in this outline. These
two great bodies will have to work constantly in unison,
the Company depending on the moral authority and support of the Society, just as the Society cannot dispense
with the material assistance of the Company. For example,
in the organizing of the clothing industry, the quantity
produced will at first be kept down so as to preserve an
equilibrium between supply and demand; and wherever the
Company undertakes the organization of new industries
the same precaution must be exercised.

But individual enterprise must never be checked by the
Company with its superior force. We shall only work
collectively when the immense difficulties of the task demand common action; we shall, wherever possible, scrupulously respect the rights of the individual. Private property,
which is the economic basis of independence, shall be developed freely and be respected by us. Our first unskilled

laborers will at once have the opportunity to work their way up to private proprietorship.

The spirit of enterprise must, indeed, be encouraged in every possible way. Organization of industries will be promoted by a judicious system of duties, by the employment of cheap raw material, and by the institution of a board to collect and publish industrial statistics.

But this spirit of enterprise must be wisely encouraged, and risky speculation must be avoided. Every new industry must be advertised for a long period before establishment, so as to prevent failure on the part of those who might wish to start a similar business six months later. Whenever a new industrial establishment is founded, the Company should be informed, so that all those interested may obtain information from it.

Industrialists will be able to make use of centralized labor agencies, which will only receive a commission large enough to ensure their continuance. The industrialists might, for example, telegraph for 500 unskilled laborers for three days, three weeks, or three months. The labor agency would then collect these 500 unskilled laborers from every possible source, and despatch them at once to carry out the agricultural or industrial enterprise. Parties of workmen will thus be systematically drafted from place to place like a body of troops. These men will, of course, not be sweated, but will work only a seven-hour day; and, in spite of their change of locality, they will preserve their organization, work out their term of service, and receive commands, promotions, and pensions. Some establishments may, of course, be able to obtain their workmen from other sources, if they wish, but they will not find it easy to do so. The Society will be able to prevent the introduction of non-Jewish work-slaves by boycotting obstinate

employers, by obstructing traffic, and by various other methods. The seven-hour workers will therefore have to be taken,
and we shall thus bring our people gradually, and without coercion, to adopt the normal seven-hour day.

SETTLEMENT OF SKILLED LABORERS

It is clear that what can be done for unskilled workers
can be even more easily done for skilled laborers. These
will work under similar regulations in the factories, and
the central labor agency will provide them when required.

Independent operatives and small employers, must be
carefully taught on account of the rapid progress of
scientific improvements, must acquire technical knowledge even if no longer very young men, must study
the power of water, and appreciate the forces of electricity. Independent workers must also be discovered and
supplied by the Society's agency. The local branch will
apply, for example, to the central office: "We want so
many carpenters, locksmiths, glaziers, etc." The central
office will publish this demand, and the proper men will
apply there for the work. These would then travel with
their families to the place where they were wanted, and
would remain there without feeling the pressure of undue
competition. A permanent and comfortable home would
thus be provided for them.

METHOD OF RAISING CAPITAL

The capital required for establishing the Company was
previously put at what seemed an absurdly high figure.
The amount actually necessary will be fixed by financiers,
and will in any case be a very considerable sum. There
are three ways of raising this sum, all of which the Society
will take under consideration. This Society, the great

"Gestor" of the Jews, will be formed by our best and most upright men, who must not derive any material advantage from their membership. Although the Society cannot at the outset possess any but moral authority, this authority will suffice to establish the credit of the Jewish Company in the nation's eyes. The Jewish Company will be unable to succeed in its enterprise unless it has received the Society's sanction; it will thus not be formed of any mere indiscriminate group of financiers. For the Society will weigh, select and decide, and will not give its approbation till it is sure of the existence of a sound basis for the conscientious carrying out of the scheme. It will not permit experiments with insufficient means, for this undertaking must succeed at the first attempt. Any initial failure would compromise the whole idea for many decades to come, or might even make its realization permanently impossible.

The three methods of raising capital are: (1) Through big banks; (2) Through small and private banks; (3) Through public subscription.

The first method of raising capital is: Through big banks. The required sum could then be raised in the shortest possible time among the large financial groups, after they had discussed the advisability of the course. The great advantage of this method would be that it would avoid the necessity of paying in the thousand millions (to keep to the original figure), immediately in its entirety. A further advantage would be that the credit of these powerful financiers would also be of service to the enterprise. Many latent political forces lie in our financial power, that power which our enemies assert to be so effective. It might be so, but actually it is not. Poor Jews feel only the hatred which this financial power provokes; its use in alleviating their lot as a body, they have not yet felt. The credit of our great Jewish financiers would have to be placed at the service of the National Idea. But should these gentlemen, who are quite satisfied with their lot, feel indisposed to do anything for their fellow-Jews who are unjustly held responsible for the large possessions of certain individuals, then the realization of this plan will afford an opportunity for drawing a clear line of distinction between them and the rest of Jewry.

The great financiers, moreover, will certainly not be asked to raise an amount so enormous out of pure philanthropic motives; that would be expecting too much. The promoters and stock holders of the Jewish Company are, on the contrary, expected to do a good piece of business, and they will be able to calculate beforehand what their chances of success are likely to be. For the Society of Jews will be in possession of all documents and references which may serve to define the prospects of the Jewish Company. The Society will in particular have investigated with exactitude the extent of the new Jewish movement, so as to provide the Company promoters with thoroughly reliable information on the amount of support they may expect. The Society will also supply the Jewish Company with comprehensive modern Jewish statistics, thus doing the work of what is called in France a "societé d'études," which undertakes all preliminary research previous to the financing of a great undertaking. Even so, the enterprise may not receive the valuable assistance of our moneyed magnates. These might, perhaps, even try to oppose the Jewish movement by means of their secret agents. Such opposition we shall meet with relentless determination.

Supposing that these magnates are content simply to turn this scheme down with a smile:

Is it, therefore, done for?

No.

For then the money will be raised in another way—by an appeal to moderately rich Jews. The smaller Jewish banks would have to be united in the name of the National Idea against the big banks till they were gathered into a second and formidable financial force. But, unfortunately, this would require a great deal of financing at first—for the £50,000,000 would have to be subscribed in full before starting work; and, as this sum could only be raised very slowly, all sorts of banking business would have to be done and loans made during the first few years. It might even occur that, in the course of all these transactions, their original object would be forgotten; the moderately rich Jews would have created a new and large business, and Jewish emigration would be forgotten.

The notion of raising money in this way is not by any means impracticable. The experiment of collecting Christian money to form an opposing force to the big banks has already been tried; that one could also oppose them with Jewish money has not been thought of until now.

But these financial conflicts would bring about all sorts of crises; the countries in which they occurred would suffer, and Anti-Semitism would become rampant.

This method is therefore not to be recommended. I have merely suggested it, because it comes up in the course of the logical development of the idea.

I also do not know whether smaller private banks would be willing to adopt it.

In any case, even the refusal of moderately rich Jews would not put an end to the scheme. On the contrary, it would then have to be taken up in real earnest.

The Society of Jews, whose members are not business

men, might try to found the Company on a national subscription.

The Company's capital might be raised, without the in-
termediary of a syndicate, by means of direct subscription
on the part of the public. Not only poor Jews, but also
Christians who wanted to get rid of them, would subscribe
a small amount to this fund. A new and peculiar form of
the plebiscite would thus be established, whereby each
man who voted for this solution of the Jewish Question
would express his opinion by subscribing a stipulated
amount. This stipulation would produce security. The funds
subscribed would only be paid in if their sum total reached
the required amount, otherwise the initial payments would
be returned.

But if the whole of the required sum is raised by popular
subscription, then each little amount would be secured by
the great numbers of other small amounts.

All this would, of course, need the express and definite
assistance of interested Governments.

IV. Local Groups

OUR TRANSMIGRATION

Previous chapters explained only how the emigration scheme might be carried out without creating any economic disturbance. But so great a movement cannot take place without inevitably rousing many deep and powerful feelings. There are old customs, old memories that attach us to our homes. We have cradles, we have graves, and we alone know how Jewish hearts cling to the graves. Our cradles we shall carry with us—they hold our future, rosy and smiling. Our beloved graves we must abandon— and I think this abandonment will cost us more than any other sacrifice. But it must be so.

Economic distress, political pressure, and social obloquy have already driven us from our homes and from our graves. We Jews are even now constantly shifting from place to place, a strong current actually carrying us westward over the sea to the United States, where our presence is also not desired. And where will our presence be desired, so long as we are a homeless nation?

But we shall give a home to our people. And we shall give it, not by dragging them ruthlessly out of their sustaining soil, but rather by transplanting them carefully to a better ground. Just as we wish to create new political and economic relations, so we shall preserve as sacred all of the past that is dear to our people's hearts.

Hence a few suggestions must suffice, as this part of my scheme will most probably be condemned as visionary. Yet even this is possible and real, though it now appears to be something vague and aimless. Organization will make of it something rational.

EMIGRATION IN GROUPS

Our people should emigrate in groups of families and friends. But no man will be forced to join the particular group belonging to his former place of residence. Each will be able to journey in his chosen fashion as soon as he has settled his affairs. Seeing that each man will pay his own expenses by rail and boat, he will naturally travel by whatever class suits him best. Possibly there will even be no subdivision for classes on board train and boat, so as to avoid making the poor feel their position too keenly during their long journey. Though we are not exactly organizing a pleasure trip, it is as well to keep them in good humor on the way.

None will travel in penury; on the other hand, all who desire to travel in luxurious ease will be able to follow their bent. Even under favorable circumstances, the movement may not touch certain classes of Jews for several years to come; the intervening period can therefore be employed in selecting the best modes of organizing the journeys. Those who are well off can travel in parties if they wish, taking their personal friends and connections with them. Jews, with the exception of the richest, have, after all, very little intercourse with Christians. In some countries their acquaintance with them is confined to a few spongers, borrowers, and dependents; of a better class of Christian they know nothing. The Ghetto continues though its walls are broken down.

The middle classes will therefore make elaborate and careful preparations for departure. A group of travellers will be formed in each locality, large towns being divided into districts with a group in each district, who will communicate by means of representatives elected for the purpose. This division into districts need not be strictly adhered to; it is merely intended to alleviate the discomfort and home-sickness of the poor during their journey outwards. Everybody is free to travel either alone or attached to any local group he prefers. The conditions of travel—regulated according to classes—will apply to all alike. Any sufficiently numerous travelling party can charter a special train and special boat from the Company.

The Company's housing agency will provide quarters for the poorest on their arrival. Later on, when more prosperous emigrants follow, their obvious need for lodgings on first landing will have to be supplied by hotels built by private enterprise. Some of these more prosperous colonists will, indeed, have built their houses before becoming permanent settlers, so that they will merely move from an old home into a new one.

It would be an affront to our intelligent elements to point out everything that they have to do. Every man who attaches himself to the National Idea will know how to spread it, and how to make it real within his sphere of influence. We shall first of all ask for the cooperation of our Rabbis.

OUR RABBIS

Every group will have its Rabbi, travelling with his congregation. Local groups will afterwards form voluntarily about their Rabbi, and each locality will have its spiritual leader. Our Rabbis, on whom we especially call, will devote their energies to the service of our idea, and will inspire their congregations by preaching it from the pulpit. They will not need to address special meetings for the purpose; an appeal such as this may be uttered in the synagogue. And thus it must be done. For we feel our historic affinity only through the faith of our fathers as we have long ago absorbed the languages of different nations to an ineradicable degree.

The Rabbis will receive communications regularly from both Society and Company, and will announce and explain these to their congregations. Israel will pray for us and for itself.

REPRESENTATIVES OF THE LOCAL GROUPS

The local groups will appoint small committees of representative men under the Rabbi's presidency, for discussion and settlement of local affairs.

Philanthropic institutions will be transferred by their local groups, each institution remaining "over there" the property of the same set of people for whom it was originally founded. I think the old buildings should not be sold, but rather devoted to the assistance of indigent Christians in the forsaken towns. The local groups will receive compensation by obtaining free building sites and every facility for reconstruction in the new country.

This transfer of philanthropic institutions will give another of those opportunities, which occur at different points of my scheme, for making an experiment in the service of humanity. Our present unsystematic private philanthropy does little good in proportion to the great expenditure it involves. But these institutions can and must form part of a system by which they will eventually supplement one another. In a new society these organizations can be evolved out of our modern consciousness, and may be based on all previous social experiments. This matter is of great importance to us, on account of our large number of paupers.

The weaker characters among us, discouraged by external pressure, spoilt by the soft-hearted charity of our rich men, easily sink until they take to begging.

The Society, supported by the local groups, will give greatest attention to popular education with regard to this particular. It will create a fruitful soil for many powers which now wither uselessly away. Whoever shows a genuine desire to work will be suitably employed. Beggars will not be endured. Whoever refuses to do anything as a free man will be sent to the workhouse.

On the other hand, we shall not relegate the old to an almshouse. An almshouse is one of the cruelest charities which our stupid good nature ever invented. There our old people die out of pure shame and mortification. There they are already buried. But we will leave even to those who stand on the lowest grade of intelligence the consoling illusion of their utility in the world. We will provide easy tasks for those who are incapable of physical labor; for we must allow for diminished vitality in the poor of an already enfeebled generation. But future generations shall be dealt with otherwise; they shall be brought up in liberty for a life of liberty.

We will seek to bestow the moral salvation of work on men of every age and of every class; and thus our people will find their strength again in the land of the seven-hour day.

PLANS OF THE TOWNS

The local groups will delegate their authorized representatives to select sites for towns. In the distribution of land every precaution will be taken to effect a careful transfer with due consideration for acquired rights.

The local groups will have plans of the towns, so that

our people may know beforehand where they are to go,
in which towns and in which houses they are to live. Comprehensive drafts of the building plans previously referred
to will be distributed among the local groups.

The principle of our administration will be strict cen-
tralization of our local groups' autonomy. In this way the
transfer will be accomplished with the minimum of pain.

I do not imagine all this to be easier than it actually is;
on the other hand, people must not imagine it to be more
difficult than it is in reality.

THE DEPARTURE OF THE MIDDLE CLASSES

The middle classes will involuntarily be drawn into the
outgoing current, for their sons will be officials of the
Society or employees of the Company "over there." Lawyers,
doctors, technicians of every description, young business
people—in fact, all Jews who are in search of opportunities, who now escape from oppression in their native
country to earn a living in foreign lands—will assemble
on a soil so full of fair promise. The daughters of the
middle classes will marry these ambitious men. One of
them will send for his wife or fiancee to come out to
him, another for his parents, brothers and sisters. Members of a new civilization marry young. This will promote general morality and ensure sturdiness in the new
generation; and thus we shall have no delicate offspring
of late marriages, children of fathers who spent their
strength in the struggle for life.

Every middle-class emigrant will draw more of his kind
after him.

The bravest will naturally get the best out of the new
world.

But there we seem undoubtedly to have touched on the crucial difficulty of my plan.

Even if we succeeded in opening a world discussion on the Jewish Question in a serious manner—

Even if this debate led us to a positive conclusion that the Jewish State were necessary to the world—

Even if the Powers assisted us in acquiring the sovereignty over a strip of territory—

How are we to transport masses of Jews without undue compulsion from their present homes to this new country?

Their emigration is surely intended to be voluntary.

THE PHENOMENON OF MULTITUDES

Great exertions will hardly be necessary to spur on the movement. Anti-Semites provide the requisite impetus. They need only do what they did before, and then they will create a desire to emigrate where it did not previously exist, and strengthen it where it existed before. Jews who now remain in Anti-Semitic countries do so chiefly because even those among them who are most ignorant of history know that numerous changes of residence in bygone centuries never brought them any permanent good. Any land which welcomed the Jews today, and offered them even fewer advantages than that which the Jewish State would guarantee them, would immediately attract a great influx of our people. The poorest, who have nothing to lose would drag themselves there. But I maintain, and every man may ask himself whether I am not right, that the pressure weighing on us arouses a desire to emigrate even among prosperous strata of society. Now our poorest strata alone would suffice to found a State; these form the strongest human material for acquiring a land, because a little despair is indispensable to the formation of a great undertaking.

But when our "desperados" increase the value of the land
by their presence and by the labor they expend on it, they
make it at the same time increasingly attractive as a place
of settlement to people who are better off.

Higher and yet higher strata will feel tempted to go over.
The expedition of the first and poorest settlers will be conducted by Company and Society conjointly, and will probably be additionally supported by existing emigration and
Zionist societies.

How may a number of people be directed to a particular
spot without being given express orders to go there? There
are certain Jewish benefactors on a large scale who try to
alleviate the sufferings of the Jews by Zionist experiments.
To them this problem also presented itself, and they thought
to solve it by giving the emigrants money or means of employment. Thus the philanthropists said: "We pay these
people to go there."

Such a procedure is utterly wrong, and all the money in
the world will not achieve its purpose.

On the other hand, the Company will say: "We shall not
pay them, we shall let them pay us. We shall merely offer
them some inducements to go."

A fanciful illustration will make my meaning more ex-
plicit: One of those philanthropists (whom we will call
"The Baron") and myself both wish to get a crowd of people
on to the plain of Longchamps near Paris, on a hot Sunday
afternoon. The Baron, by promising them 10 francs each,
will, for 200,000 francs, bring out 20,000 perspiring and
miserable people, who will curse him for having given them
so much annoyance. Whereas I will offer these 200,000 francs
as a prize for the swiftest racehorse—and then I shall have
to put up barriers to keep the people off Longchamps. They
will pay to go in: 1 franc, 5 francs, 20 francs.

The consequence will be that I shall get the half-a-million of people out there; the President of the Republic will drive up "a la Daumont"; and the crowds will enjoy and amuse themselves. Most of them will think it an agreeable walk in the open air in spite of heat and dust; and I shall have made by my 200,000 francs about a million in entrance money and taxes on gaming. I shall get the same people out there whenever I like but the Baron will not—not on any account.

I will give a more serious illustration of the phenomenon of multitudes where they are earning a livelihood. Let any man attempt to cry through the streets of a town: "Whoever is willing to stand all day long through a winter's terrible cold, through a summer's tormenting heat, in an iron hall exposed on all sides, there to address every passer-by, and to offer him fancy wares, or fish, or fruit, will receive two florins, or four francs or something similar."

How many people would go to the hall? How many days would they hold out when hunger drove them there? And if they held out, what energy would they display in trying to persuade passers-by to buy fish, fruit and fancy wares?

We shall set about it in a different way. In places where trade is active, and these places we shall the more easily discover, since we ourselves direct trade withersoever we wish, in these places we shall build large halls, and call them markets. These halls might be worse built and more unwholesome than those above mentioned, and yet people would stream towards them. But we shall use our best efforts, and we shall build them better, and make them more beautiful than the first. And the people, to whom we had promised nothing, because we cannot promise anything without deceiving them, these excellent, keen business men will gaily create most active commercial intercourse. They will harangue the buyers unweariedly; they will stand on their feet, and scarcely think of fatigue. They will hurry off at dawn, so as to be first on the spot; they will form unions, cartels, anything to continue bread-winning undisturbed. And if they find at the end of the day that all their hard work has produced only 1 florin, 50 kreutzer, or 3 francs, or something similar, they will yet look forward hopefully to the next day, which may, perhaps, bring them better luck.

We have given them hope.

Would any one ask whence the demand comes which creates the market? Is it really necessary to tell them again?

I pointed out that by means of the system "Assistance par le Travail" the return could be increased fifteenfold. One million would produce fifteen millions; and one thousand millions, fifteen thousand millions.

This may be the case on a small scale; is it so on a large one? Capital surely yields a return diminishing in inverse ratio to its own growth. Inactive and inert capital yields this diminishing return, but active capital brings in a marvellously increasing return. Herein lies the social question.

Am I stating a fact? I call on the richest Jews as witnesses of my veracity. Why do they carry on so many different industries? Why do they send men to work underground and to raise coal amid terrible dangers for meagre pay? I cannot imagine this to be pleasant, even for the owners of the mines. For I do not believe that capitalists are heartless, and I do not pretend that I believe it. My desire is not to accentuate, but to smooth differences.

Is it necessary to illustrate the phenomenon of multitudes, and their concentration on a particular spot by references to pious pilgrimages?

I do not want to hurt anyone's religious sensibility by words which might be wrongly interpreted.

I shall merely refer quite briefly to the Mohammedan

pilgrimages to Mecca, the Catholic pilgrimages to Lourdes, and to many other spots whence men return comforted by their faith, and to the holy Hock at Trier. Thus we shall also create a center for the deep religious needs of our people. Our ministers will understand us first, and will be with us in this.

We shall let every man find salvation "over there" in his own particular way. Above and before all we shall make room for the immortal band of our Freethinkers, who are continually making new conquests for humanity.

No more force will be exercised on any one than is necessary for the preservation of the State and order; and the requisite force will not be arbitrarily defined by one or more shifting authorities; it will be fixed by iron laws.

Now, if the illustrations I gave make people draw the inference that a multitude can be only temporarily attracted to centers of faith, of business, or of amusement, the reply to their objection is simple. Whereas one of these objects by itself would certainly only attract the masses, all these centers of attraction combined would be calculated permanently to hold and satisfy them. For all these centers together form a single, great, long-sought object, which our people has always longed to attain, for which it has kept itself alive, for which it has been kept alive by external pressure—a free home! When the movement commences, we shall draw some men after us and let others follow; others again will be swept into the current, and the last will be thrust after us.

These last hesitating settlers will be the worst off, both here and there.

But the first, who go over with faith, enthusiasm, and courage will have the best positions.

OUR HUMAN MATERIAL

There are more mistaken notions abroad concerning
Jews than concerning any other people. And we have
become so depressed and discouraged by our historic sufferings that we 'ourselves repeat and believe these mistakes.
One of these is that we have an immoderate love of
business. Now it is well known that wherever we are
permitted to take part in the rising of classes, we give
up our business as soon as possible. The great majority of
Jewish business men give their sons a superior education.
Hence, the so-called "Judaizing" of all intellectual pro-
fessions. But even in economically feebler grades of
society, our love of trade is not so predominant as is generally supposed. In the Eastern countries of Europe there
are great numbers of Jews who are not traders, and who
are not afraid of hard work either. The Society of Jews
will be in a position to prepare scientifically accurate statistics of our human forces. The new tasks and prospects
that await our people in the new country will satisfy our
present handicraftsmen, and will transform many present
small traders into manual workers.

A peddler who travels about the country with a heavy
pack on his back is not so contented as his persecutors imagine. The seven-hour day will convert all of his kind
into workmen. They are good, misunderstood people, who
now suffer perhaps more severely than any others. The
Society of Jews will, moreover, busy itself from the outset
with their training as artisans. Their love of gain will be
encouraged in a healthy manner. Jews are of a thrifty
and adaptable disposition, and are qualified for any means
of earning a living, and it will therefore suffice to make
small trading unremunerative, to cause even present peddlers to give it up altogether. This could be brought about,

for example, by encouraging large department stores which provide all necessaries of life. These general stores are already crushing small trading in large cities. In a land of new civilization they will absolutely prevent its existence. The establishment of these stores is further advantageous, because it makes the country immediately habitable for people who require more refined necessaries of life.

HABITS

Is a reference to the little habits and comforts of the ordinary man in keeping with the serious nature of this pamphlet?

I think it is in keeping, and, moreover, very important. For these little habits are the thousand and one fine delicate threads which together go to make up an unbreakable rope.

Here certain limited notions must be set aside. Whoever has seen anything of the world knows that just these little daily customs can easily be transplanted everywhere. The technical contrivances of our day, which this scheme intends to employ in the service of humanity, have heretofore been principally used for our little habits. There are English hotels in Egypt and on the mountain-crest in Switzerland, Vienna cafes in South Africa, French theatres in Russia, German operas in America, and best Bavarian beer in Paris.

When we journey out of Egypt again we shall not leave the fleshpots behind.

Every man will find his customs again in the local groups, but they will be better, more beautiful, and more agreeable than before.

V. Society of Jews and Jewish State

NEGOTIORUM GESTIO

T HIS PAMPHLET IS NOT INTENDED FOR LAWYERS. I CAN therefore touch only cursorily, as on so many other things, upon my theory of the legal basis of a State.

I must, nevertheless, lay some stress on my new theory, which could be maintained, I believe, even in discussion with men well versed in jurisprudence.

According to Rousseau's now antiquated view, a State is formed by a social contract. Rousseau held that: "The conditions of this contract are so precisely defined by the nature of the agreement that the slightest alteration would make them null and void. The consequence is that, even where they are not expressly stated, they are everywhere identical, and everywhere tacitly accepted and recognized," etc.

A logical and historic refutation of Rousseau's theory was never, nor is now, difficult, however terrible and far-reaching its effects may have been. The question whether a social contract with "conditions not expressly stated, yet unalterable," existed before the framing of a constitution, is of no practical interest to States under modern forms of government. The legal relationship between government and citizen is in any case clearly established now.

But previous to the framing of a constitution, and during the creation of a new State, these principles assume great practical importance. We know and see for ourselves that States still continue to be created. Colonies secede from the mother country. Vassals fall away from

136

their suzerain; newly opened territories are immediately formed into free States. It is true that the Jewish State is conceived as a peculiarly modern structure on unspecified territory. But a State is formed, not by pieces of land, but rather by a number of men united under sovereign rule.

The people is the subjective, land the objective foundation of a State, and the subjective basis is the more important of the two. One sovereignty, for example, which has no objective basis at all, is perhaps the most respected one in the world. I refer to the sovereignty of the Pope.

The theory of rationality is the one at present accepted in political science. This theory suffices to justify the creation of a State, and cannot be historically refuted in the same way as the theory of a contract. Insofar as I am concerned only with the creation of a Jewish State, I am well within the limits of the theory of rationality. But when I touch upon the legal basis of the State, I have exceeded them. The theories of a divine institution, or of superior power, or of a contract, and the patriarchal and patrimonial theories do not accord with modern views. The legal basis of a State is sought either too much within men (patriarchal theory, and theories of superior force and contract), or too far above them (divine institution), or too far below them (objective patrimonial theory). The theory of rationality leaves this question conveniently and carefully unanswered. But a question which has seriously occupied doctors of jurisprudence in every age cannot be an absolutely idle one. As a matter of fact, a mixture of human and superhuman goes to the making of a State. Some legal basis is indispensable to explain the somewhat oppressive relationship in which subjects occasionally stand to rulers. I believe it is to be found in the *negotiorum gestio,* wherein the body of citizens represents the *dominus negotiorum,* and the government represents the *gestor.*

The Romans, with their marvellous sense of justice, produced that noble masterpiece, the *negotiorum gestio.* When the property of an oppressed person is in danger, any man may step forward to save it. This man is the *gestor,* the director of affairs not strictly his own. He has received no warrant—that is, no human warrant; higher obligations authorize him to act. The higher obligations may be formulated in different ways for the State, and so as to respond to individual degrees of culture attained by a growing general power of comprehension. The *gestio* is intended to work for the good of the *dominus* —the people, to whom the *gestor* himself belongs.

The *gestor* administers property of which he is joint-owner. His joint proprietorship teaches him what urgency would warrant his intervention, and would demand his leadership in peace or war; but under no circumstances is his authority valid *qua* joint proprietorship. The consent of the numerous joint-owners is even under most favorable conditions a matter of conjecture.

A State is created by a nation's struggle for existence. In any such struggle it is impossible to obtain proper authority in circumstantial fashion beforehand. In fact, any previous attempt to obtain a regular decision from the majority would probably ruin the undertaking from the outset. For internal schisms would make the people defenceless against external dangers. We cannot all be of one mind; the *gestor* will therefore simply take the leadership into his hands and march in the van.

The action of the *gestor* of the State is sufficiently warranted if the common cause is in danger, and the *dominus* is prevented, either by want of will or by some other reason, from helping itself.

But the *gestor* becomes similar to the *dominus* by his intervention, and is bound by the agreement *quasi ex contractu*. This is the legal relationship existing before, or, more correctly, created simultaneously with the State.

The *gestor* thus becomes answerable for every form of negligence, even for the failure of business undertakings, and the neglect of such affairs as are intimately connected with them, etc. I shall not further enlarge on the *negotiorum gestio*, but rather leave it to the State, else it would take us too far from the main subject. One remark only: "Business management, if it is approved by the owner, is just as effectual as if it had originally been carried on by his authority."

And how does all this affect our case?

The Jewish people are at present prevented by the Diaspora from conducting their political affairs themselves. Besides, they are in a condition of more or less severe distress in many parts of the world. They need, above all things a *gestor*. This *gestor* cannot, of course, be a single individual. Such a one would either make himself ridiculous, or—seeing that he would appear to be working for his own interests—contemptible.

The *gestor* of the Jews must therefore be a body corporate.

And that is the Society of Jews. *manager of political affairs*

THE GESTOR OF THE JEWS

This organ of the national movement, the nature and functions of which we are at last dealing with, will, in fact, be created before everything else. Its formation is perfectly simple. It will take shape among those energetic Jews to whom I imparted my scheme in London.*

The Society will have scientific and political tasks, for the founding of a Jewish State, as I conceive it, presupposes the application of scientific methods. We cannot journey out of Egypt today in the primitive fashion of ancient times. We shall previously obtain an accurate account of our number and strength. The undertaking of that great and ancient *gestor* of the Jews in primitive days bears much the same relation to ours that some wonderful melody bears to a modern opera. We are playing the same melody with many more violins, flutes, harps, violoncellos, and bass viols; with electric light, decorations, choirs, beautiful costumes, and with the first singers of their day.

This pamphlet is intended to open a general discussion on the Jewish Question. Friends and foes will take part in it; but it will no longer, I hope, take the form of violent abuse or of sentimental vindication, but of a debate, practical, large, earnest, and political.

The Society of Jews will gather all available declarations of statesmen, parliaments, Jewish communities, societies, whether expressed in speeches or writings, in meetings, newspapers or books.

Thus the Society will find out for the first time whether the Jews really wish to go to the Promised Land, and whether they must go there. Every Jewish community in the world will send contributions to the Society towards a comprehensive collection of Jewish statistics.

Further tasks, such as investigation by experts of the new country and its natural resources, the uniform planning of migration and settlement, preliminary work for

---

* Dr. Herzl addressed a meeting of the Maccabean Club, at which Israel Zangwill presided, on November 24th, 1895.

legislation and administration, etc., must be rationally evolved out of the original scheme.

Externally, the Society will attempt, as I explained before in the general part, to be acknowledged as a State-forming power. The free assent of many Jews will confer on it the requisite authority in its relations with Governments.

Internally, that is to say, in its relation with the Jewish people, the Society will create all the first indispensable institutions; it will be the nucleus out of which the public institutions of the Jewish State will later on be developed.

Our first object is, as I said before, supremacy, assured to us by international law, over a portion of the globe sufficiently large to satisfy our just requirements.

What is the next step?

THE OCCUPATION OF THE LAND

When nations wandered in historic times, they let chance carry them, draw them, fling them hither and thither, and like swarms of locusts they settled down indifferently anywhere. For in historic times the earth was not known to man. But this modern Jewish migration must proceed in accordance with scientific principles.

Not more than forty years ago gold-digging was carried on in an extraordinarily primitive fashion. What adventurous days were those in California! A report brought desperados together from every quarter of the earth; they stole pieces of land, robbed each other of gold, and finally gambled it away, as robbers do.

But today! What is gold-digging like in the Transvaal today? Adventurous vagabonds are not there; sedate geologists and engineers alone are on the spot to regulate its gold industry, and to employ ingenious machinery in separating the ore from surrounding rock. Little is left to chance now.

Thus we must investigate and take possession of the new Jewish country by means of every modern expedient.

As soon as we have secured the land, we shall send over a ship, having on board the representatives of the Society, of the Company, and of the local groups, who will enter into possession at once.

These men will have three tasks to perform: (1) An accurate, scientific investigation of all natural resources of the country; (2) the organization of a strictly centralized administration; (3) the distribution of land. These tasks intersect one another, and will all be carried out in conformity with the now familiar object in view.

One thing remains to be explained—namely, how the occupation of land according to local groups is to take place.

In America the occupation of newly opened territory is set about in naive fashion. The settlers assemble on the frontier, and at the appointed time make a simultaneous and violent rush for their portions.

We shall not proceed thus to the new land of the Jews. The lots in provinces and towns will be sold by auction, and paid for, not in money, but in work. The general plan will have settled on streets, bridges, waterworks, etc., necessary for traffic. These will be united into provinces. Within these provinces sites for towns will be similarly sold by auction. The local groups will pledge themselves to carry the business property through, and will cover the cost by means of self-imposed assessments. The Society will be in a position to judge whether the local groups are not venturing on sacrifices too great for their means. The large communities will receive large sites for their activity. Great

orderly, regulated occupation

sacrifices will thus be rewarded by the establishment of universities, technical schools, academies, research institutes, etc., and these Government institutes, which do not have to be concentrated in the capital, will be distributed over the country.

The personal interest of the buyers, and, if necessary, the local assessment, will guarantee the proper working of what has been taken over. In the same way, as we cannot, and indeed do not wish to obliterate distinctions between single individuals, so the differences between local groups will also continue. Everything will shape itself quite naturally. All acquired rights will be protected, and every new development will be given sufficient scope.

Our people will be made thoroughly acquainted with all these matters.

We shall not take others unawares or mislead them, any more than we shall deceive ourselves.

Everything must be systematically settled beforehand. I merely indicate this scheme: our keenest thinkers will combine in elaborating it. Every social and technical achievement of our age and of the more advanced age which will be reached before the slow execution of my plan is accomplished must be employed for this object. Every valuable invention which exists now, or lies in the future, must be used. By these means a country can be occupied and a State founded in a manner as yet unknown to history, and with possibilities of success such as never occurred before.

CONSTITUTION

One of the great commissions which the Society will have to appoint will be the council of State jurists. These must formulate the best, that is, the best modern constitution possible. I believe that a good constitution should be of moderately elastic nature. In another work I have explained in detail what forms of government I hold to be the best. I think a democratic monarchy and an aristocratic republic are the finest forms of a State, because in them the form of State and the principle of government are opposed to each other, and thus preserve a true balance of power. I am a staunch supporter of monarchial institutions, because these allow of a continuous policy, and represent the interests of a historically famous family born and educated to rule, whose desires are bound up with the preservation of the State. But our history has been too long interrupted for us to attempt direct continuity of ancient constitutional forms, without exposing ourselves to the charge of absurdity.

A democracy without a sovereign's useful counterpoise is extreme in appreciation and condemnation, tends to idle discussion in Parliaments, and produces that objectionable class of men—professional politicians. Nations are also really not fit for unlimited democracy at present, and will become less and less fitted for it in the future. For a pure democracy presupposes a predominance of simple customs, and our customs become daily more complex with the growth of commerce and increase of culture. *"Le ressort d'une democratie est la vertu,"* said wise Montesquieu. And where is this virtue, that is to say, this political virtue, to be met with? I do not believe in our political virtue; first, because we are no better than the rest of modern humanity; and, secondly, because freedom will make us show our fighting qualities at first. I also hold a settling of questions by the referendum to be an unsatisfactory procedure, because there are no simple political questions which can be answered merely by Yes and No. The masses are also more prone even than Parliaments to be led away by heterodox opinions, and to be swayed by vigorous ranting. It is impossible to formulate a wise internal or external policy in a popular assembly.

Politics must take shape in the upper strata and work downwards. But no member of the Jewish State will be oppressed, every man will be able and will wish to rise in it. Thus a great upward tendency will pass through our people; every individual by trying to raise himself, raising also the whole body of citizens. The ascent will take a normal form, useful to the State and serviceable to the National Idea.

Hence I incline to an aristocratic republic. This would satisfy the ambitious spirit in our people, which has now degenerated into petty vanity. Many of the institutions of Venice pass through my mind; but all that which caused the ruin of Venice must be carefully avoided. We shall learn from the historic mistakes of others, in the same way as we learn from our own; for we are a modern nation, and wish to be the most modern in the world. Our people, who are receiving the new country from the Society, will also thankfully accept the new constitution it offers them. Should any opposition manifest itself, the Society will suppress it. The Society cannot permit the exercise of its functions to be interpreted by short-sighted or ill-disposed individuals. *Is there no political free speech?*

LANGUAGE

It might be suggested that our want of a common current language would present difficulties. We cannot converse with one another in Hebrew. Who amongst us has a sufficient acquaintance with Hebrew to ask for a railway ticket in that language? Such a thing cannot be done.

Yet the difficulty is very easily circumvented. Every man can preserve the language in which his thoughts are at home. Switzerland affords a conclusive proof of the possibility of a federation of tongues. We shall remain in the new country what we now are here, and we shall never cease to cherish with sadness the memory of the native land out of which we have been driven.

We shall give up using those miserable stunted jargons, those Ghetto languages which we still employ, for these were the stealthy tongues of prisoners. Our national teachers will give due attention to this matter; and the language which proves itself to be of greatest utility for general intercourse will be adopted without compulsion as our national tongue. Our community of race is peculiar and unique, for we are bound together only by the faith of our fathers.

THEOCRACY

Shall we end by having a theocracy? No, indeed. Faith unites us, knowledge gives us freedom. We shall therefore prevent any theocratic tendencies from coming to the fore on the part of our priesthood. We shall keep our priests within the confines of their temples in the same way as we shall keep our professional army within the confines of their barracks. Army and priesthood shall receive honors high as their valuable functions deserve. But they must not interfere in the administration of the State which confers distinction upon them, else they will conjure up difficulties without and within.

Every man will be as free and undisturbed in his faith or his disbelief as he is in his nationality. And if it should occur that men of other creeds and different nationalities come to live amongst us, we should accord them honorable protection and equality before the law. We have learnt toleration in Europe. This is not sarcastically said; for the Anti-Semitism of today could only in a very few places be taken for old religious intolerance. It is for the most part a movement among civilized nations by which they try to chase away the spectres of their own past.

LAWS

When the idea of a State begins to approach realization, the Society of Jews will appoint a council of jurists to do the preparatory work of legislation. During the transition period these must act on the principle that every emigrant *what?* Jew is to be judged according to the laws of the country which he has left. But they must try to bring about a unification of these various laws to form a modern system of legislation based on the best portions of previous systems. This might become a typical codification, embodying all the just social claims of the present day.

THE ARMY

The Jewish State is conceived as a neutral one. It will therefore require only a professional army, equipped, of course, with every requisite of modern warfare, to preserve order internally and externally.

THE FLAG

We have no flag, and we need one. If we desire to lead many men, we must raise a symbol above their heads.

I would suggest a white flag, with seven golden stars. The white field symbolizes our pure new life; the stars are the seven golden hours of our working-day. For we shall march into the Promised Land carrying the badge of honor.

RECIPROCITY AND EXTRADITION TREATIES

The new Jewish State must be properly founded, with due regard to our future honorable position in the world. Therefore every obligation in the old country must be scrupulously fulfilled before leaving. The Society of Jews and the Jewish Company will grant cheap passage and certain advantages in settlement to those only who can present an official testimonial from the local authorities, certifying that they have left their affairs in good order.

Every just private claim originating in the abandoned countries will be heard more readily in the Jewish State than anywhere else. We shall not wait for reciprocity; we shall act purely for the sake of our own honor. We shall thus perhaps find, later on, that law courts will be more willing to hear our claims than now seems to be the case in some places.

It will be inferred, as a matter of course, from previous remarks, that we shall deliver up Jewish criminals more readily than any other State would do, till the time comes when we can enforce our penal code on the same principles as every other civilized nation does. There will therefore be a period of transition, during which we shall receive our criminals only after they have suffered due penalties. But, having made amends, they will be received without any restrictions whatever, for our criminals also must enter upon a new life.

Thus emigration may become to many Jews a crisis with a happy issue. Bad external circumstances, which ruin many a character, will be removed, and this change may mean salvation to many who are lost.

Here I should like briefly to relate a story I came across in an account of the gold mines of Witwatersrand. One day a man came to the Rand, settled there, tried his hand at various things, with the exception of gold mining, till he founded an ice factory, which did well. He soon won universal esteem by his respectability, but after some years he was suddenly arrested. He had committed some defalcations as banker in Frankfort, had fled from there, and had begun a new life under an assumed name. But when he was led away as prisoner, the most respected people in the place appeared at the station, bade him a cordial farewell and *au revoir*—for he was certain to return.

How much this story reveals! A new life can regenerate even criminals, and we have a proportionately small number of these. Some interesting statistics on this point are worth reading, entitled "The Criminality of Jews in Germany," by Dr. P. Nathan, of Berlin, who was commissioned by the "Society for Defense against Anti-Semitism" to make a collection of statistics based on official returns. It is true that this pamphlet, which teems with figures, has been prompted, as many another "defence," by the error that Anti-Semitism can be refuted by reasonable arguments. We are probably disliked as much for our gifts as we are for our faults.

BENEFITS OF THE EMIGRATION OF THE JEWS

I imagine that Governments will, either voluntarily or under pressure from the Anti-Semites, pay certain attention to this scheme, and they may perhaps actually receive it here and there with a sympathy which they will also show to the Society of Jews.

For the emigration which I suggest will not create any economic crises. Such crises as would follow everywhere in consequence of Jew-baiting would rather be prevented by the carrying out of my plan. A great period of prosperity would commence in countries which are now Anti-

economic crises will be averted as Christians take over businesses + jobs vacated by Jews

Semitic. For there will be, as I have repeatedly said, an internal migration of Christian citizens into the positions slowly and systematically evacuated by the Jews. If we are not merely suffered, but actually assisted to do this, the movement will have a generally beneficial effect. That is a narrow view, from which one should free oneself, which sees in the departure of many Jews a consequent impoverishment of countries. It is different from a departure which is a result of persecution, for then property is indeed destroyed, as it is ruined in the confusion of war. Different again is the peaceable voluntary departure of colonists, wherein everything is carried out with due consideration for acquired rights, and with absolute conformity to law, openly and by light of day, under the eyes of the authorities and the control of public opinion. The emigration of Christian proletarians to different parts of the world would be brought to a standstill by the Jewish movement.

The States would have a further advantage in the enormous increase of their export trade; for, since the emigrant Jews "over there" would depend for a long time to come on European productions, they would necessarily have to import them. The local groups would keep up a just balance, and the customary needs would have to be supplied for a long time at the accustomed places.

Another, and perhaps one of the greatest advantages, would be the ensuing social relief. Social dissatisfaction would be appeased during the twenty or more years which the emigration of the Jews would occupy, and would in any case be set at rest during the whole transition period.

The shape which the social question may take depends entirely on the development of our technical resources. Steampower concentrated men in factories about machinery where they were overcrowded, and where they made one another miserable by overcrowding. Our present enormous, injudicious, and unsystematic rate of production is the cause of continual severe crises which ruin both employers and employees. Steam crowded men together; electricity will probably scatter them again, and may perhaps bring about a more prosperous condition of the labor market. In any case our technical inventors, who are the true benefactors of humanity, will continue their labors after the commencement of the emigration of the Jews, and they will discover things as marvellous as those we have already seen, or indeed more wonderful even than these.

The word "impossible" has ceased to exist in the vocabulary of technical science. Were a man who lived in the last century to return to the earth, he would find the life of today full of incomprehensible magic. Wherever the moderns appear with our inventions, we transform the desert into a garden. To build a city takes in our time as many years as it formerly required centuries; America offers endless examples of this. Distance has ceased to be an obstacle. The spirit of our age has gathered fabulous treasures into its storehouse. Every day this wealth increases. A hundred thousand heads are occupied with speculations and research at every point of the globe, and what any one discovers belongs the next moment to the whole world. We ourselves will use and carry on every new attempt in our Jewish land; and just as we shall introduce the seven-hour day as an experiment for the good of humanity, so we shall proceed in everything else in the same humane spirit, making of the new land a land of experiments and a model State.

After the departure of the Jews the undertakings which they have created will remain where they originally were found. And the Jewish spirit of enterprise will not even fail where people welcome it. For Jewish capitalists will be glad to invest their funds where they are familiar with surrounding conditions. And whereas Jewish money is now sent out of countries on account of existing persecutions, and is sunk in most distant foreign undertakings, it will flow back again in consequence of this peaceable solution, and will contribute to the further progress of the countries which the Jews have left.

VI. Conclusion

HOW MUCH HAS BEEN LEFT UNEXPLAINED, HOW MANY defects, how many harmful superficialities, and how many useless repetitions in this pamphlet, which I have thought over so long and so often revised!

But a fair-minded reader, who has sufficient understanding to grasp the spirit of my words, will not be repelled by these defects. He will rather be roused thereby to cooperate with his intelligence and energy in a work which is not one man's task alone, and to improve it.

Have I not explained obvious things and overlooked important objections?

I have tried to meet certain objections; but I know that many more will be made, based on high grounds and low.

To the first class of objections belongs the remark that the Jews are not the only people in the world who are in a condition of distress. Here I would reply that we may as well begin by removing a little of this misery, even if it should at first be no more than our own.

It might further be said that we ought not to create new distinctions between people; we ought not to raise fresh barriers, we should rather make the old disappear. But men who think in this way are amiable visionaries; and the idea of a native land will still flourish when the dust of their bones will have vanished tracelessly in the winds. Universal brotherhood is not even a beautiful dream. Antagonism is essential to man's greatest efforts.

But the Jews, once settled in their own State, would probably have no more enemies. As for those who remain behind, since prosperity enfeebles and causes them to dimin-

ish, they would soon disappear altogether. I think the Jews
will always have sufficient enemies, such as every nation
has. But once fixed in their own land, it will no longer be
possible for them to scatter all over the world. The diaspora
cannot be reborn, unless the civilization of the whole earth
should collapse; and such a consummation could be feared
by none but foolish men. Our present civilization possesses
weapons powerful enough for its self-defence.

Innumerable objections will be based on low grounds,
for there are more low men than noble in this world. I
have tried to remove some of these narrow-minded notions;
and whoever is willing to fall in behind our white flag
with its seven stars, must assist in this campaign of enlightenment. Perhaps we shall have to fight first of all against
many an evil-disposed, narrow-hearted, short-sighted member of our own race.

Again, people will say that I am furnishing the Anti-
Semites with weapons. Why so? Because I admit the
truth? Because I do not maintain that there are none but
excellent men amongst us?

Will not people say that I am showing our enemies the
way to injure us? This I absolutely dispute. My proposal
could only be carried out with the free consent of a majority of Jews. Action may be taken against individuals or
even against groups of the most powerful Jews, but Governments will never take action against all Jews. The equal
rights of the Jew before the law cannot be withdrawn
where they have once been conceded; for the first attempt
at withdrawal would immediately drive all Jews, rich and
poor alike, into the ranks of revolutionary parties. The
beginning of any official acts of injustice against the Jews
invariably brings about economic crises. Therefore, no
weapons can be effectually used against us, because these

injure the hands that wield them. Meantime hatred grows apace. The rich do not feel it much, but our poor do. Let us ask our poor, who have been more severely proletarized since the last removal of Anti-Semitism than ever before.

Some of our prosperous men may say that the pressure is not yet severe enough to justify emigration, and that every forcible expulsion shows how unwilling our people are to depart. True, because they do not know where to go; because they only pass from one trouble into another. But we are showing them the way to the Promised Land; and the splendid force of enthusiasm must fight against the terrible force of habit.

Persecutions are no longer so malignant as they were in the Middle Ages? True, but our sensitiveness has increased, so that we feel no diminution in our sufferings; prolonged persecution has overstrained our nerves.

Will people say, again, that our enterprise is hopeless, because even if we obtained the land with supremacy over it, the poor only would go with us? It is precisely the poorest whom we need at first. Only the desperate make good conquerors.

Will some one say: Were it feasible it would have been done long ago?

It has never yet been possible; now it is possible. A hundred—or even fifty years ago it would have been nothing more than a dream. Today it may become a reality. Our rich, who have a pleasurable acquaintance with all our technical achievements, know full well how much money can do. And thus it will be: just the poor and simple, who do not know what power man already exercises over the forces of Nature, just these will have the firmest faith in the new message. For these have never lost their hope of the Promised Land.

Here it is, fellow Jews! Neither fable nor deception! Every man may test its reality for himself, for every man will carry over with him a portion of the Promised Land— one in his head, another in his arms, another in his acquired possessions.

Now, all this may appear to be an interminably long affair. Even in the most favorable circumstances, many years might elapse before the commencement of the foundation of the State. In the meantime, Jews in a thousand different places would suffer insults, mortifications, abuse, blows, depredation, and death. No; if we only begin to carry out the plans, Anti-Semitism would stop at once and for ever. For it is the conclusion of peace.

The news of the formation of our Jewish Company will be carried in a single day to the remotest ends of the earth by the lightning speed of our telegraph wires.

And immediate relief will ensue. The intellects which we produce so superabundantly in our middle classes will find an outlet in our first organizations, as our first technicians, officers, professors, officials, lawyers, and doctors; and thus the movement will continue in swift but smooth progression.

Prayers will be offered up for the success of our work in temples and in churches also; for it will bring relief from an old burden, which all have suffered.

But we must first bring enlightenment to men's minds. The idea must make its way into the most distant, miserable holes where our people dwell. They will awaken from gloomy brooding, for into their lives will come a new significance. Every man need think only of himself, and the movement will assume vast proportions.

And what glory awaits those who fight unselfishly for the cause!

Therefore I believe that a wondrous generation of Jews

will spring into existence. The Maccabeans will rise again.

Let me repeat once more my opening words: The Jews who wish for a State will have it.

We shall live at last as free men on our own soil, and die peacefully in our own homes.

The world will be freed by our liberty, enriched by our wealth, magnified by our greatness.

And whatever we attempt there to accomplish for our own welfare, will react powerfully and beneficially for the good of humanity.

BIBLIOGRAPHY

THE CONGRESS ADDRESSES. New York, Federation of American Zionists, 1917. 40p.

EXCERPTS FROM HERZL'S DIARIES. New York, Scopus pub. co. 1941. 122p.

GESAMELTE SHRIFTEN (In Yiddish). New York, Literarishe Verlag, 1920. 2 vols.

GESAMMELTE ZIONISTISCHE WERKE. 3rd ed. Berlin. Juedisher Verlag (1934) 5 vols. Contents: vol. 1 Zionistische shriften; vol. 2, 3, 4, Taegebuecher, vol. 5 Das neue Ghetto; Altneuland, Aus dem Nachlass.

DAS JUDENSTAAT; Versuch einer modernen Lösung der Judenfrage. Neue Auflage mit einem Vorwort von Otto Warburg. Berlin, Juedischer Verlag, 1918. 88p.
Various editions.

OLD-NEW LAND tr. by Lotta Levensohn with a preface by Stephen S. Wise. New York, Bloch pub. co. 1941. 296p.

THE TRAGEDY OF JEWISH IMMIGRATION. 2nd ed. New York, Zionist organization of America, 1920. 47p.

ABOUT THEODOR HERZL

Bein, Alex. Theodore Herzl tr. by Maurice Samuel. Phil. Jewish. pub. society, 1940. 545p.

Brainin, Ruben. A Life of Herzl. Vol. 1, New York, 1919. (Hebrew)

Buber, Martin and Weltsch, Robert. Theodor Herzl and we. New York, Hitachduth of America, 1929. 28p.

De Haas, Jacob. Theodor Herzl, a biographical study. New York, 1927. 2 vols.

Hoffman, Martha. The young Herzl (In Hebrew) Jerusalem, 1941. 103p.

Neumann, Emanuel. The birth of statesmanship; a story of Theodor Herzl's life, New York, Youth dept. Jewish National Fund of America. 48p.

New Palestine. Theodor Herzl, a memorial; ed. by Meyer W. Weisgal. New York, 1929. 320p.

Zionist Organization Executive. Theodor Herzl, ein Gedenkbuch. Berlin, Juedischer Verlag, 1929. 79p.

CHRONOLOGY

1860—May 2	Wolf Theodor (Benjamin Zev) Herzl is born in the Tabakgasse, Budapest, the son of Jakob and Jeanette (Diamant) Herzl.
1885—May 27	First feuilleton published in Wiener Allgemeine Zeitung.
1894—Oct. 21	Arrest of Dreyfus.
Oct. 21-Nov. 8	Writes Das Neue Ghetto. This is an attempt to express himself on the Jewish question.
1895—June 2	Interviews Baron de Hirsch, submits plan for political action. Not favorably received. Immediately after this interview, which he later designates the beginning of his Zionist work, Herzl begins his Diaries.
June-July	Composes first draft of Der Judenstaat.
November 17	Explains idea of Jewish State to Dr. Nordau in Paris. Meets with instant understanding. Nordau gives Herzl introduction to Zangwill and London Maccabean Club.
November 21	London. First meeting with Zangwill.
1895—Nov. 24	London. First address before Maccabean Club.
1896—Feb. 14	Der Judenstaat published in Vienna.
May	Herzl recognized as leader by Zionist students of Vienna.
July 13	London. Proclaimed leader of Jewry at meeting of Whitechapel Jews. Conflict with Chovevei Zion.
July 18	Paris. Meeting with Baron Edmond Rothschild, who considers plan impracticable.
November 8	Writes to British Zionists suggesting collection of a national fund.
1897—March 6	Zionsverein decides upon Zionist Congress in Munich on August 25.
June 4	Publication of first issue of Die Welt.
June 17	Zionist Actions Committee decides to hold Congress in Basle.
Aug. 29-31	First Zionist Congress convenes in Basle.

159

1898—Aug. 28-30   Second Zionist Congress meets at Basle.

October 26   Herzl party lands at Jaffa; tours Jewish colonies of Palestine.

November 2   Formal audience with German Emperor at his headquarters outside Jerusalem. Problems of colonization discussed.

1899—March 20   Registration of name of Jewish Colonial Trust, Ltd.

August 15-17   Third Zionist Congress held at Basle.

1900—Aug. 2   Fourth Zionist Congress opens in London. Herzl attends though he has barely recovered from serious illness.

1901—May 18   Formal audience with Abdul Hamid II at Yildiz Kiosk. Herzl is promised pro-Jewish proclamation. Receives Grand Cordon of the Order of Medjidje, First Class.

Dec. 29-31   Fifth Congress convenes at Basle. Zangwill attacks ICA. Conflict between Herzl and Russian "cultural" Zionists. Discussion of National Fund.

1902—Feb. 17   Constantinople. Sultan offers Herzl charter, but not for Palestine.

July 5   London. Conference with Lord Rothschild.

July 7   London. Herzl appears before Royal Commission on Alien Immigration.

October   Publication of Altneuland.

1903—Jan.   El Arish expedition organized.

May 11   Permission for El Arish colonization refused by Egypt.

August 16   Vilna. Great ovations. There receives letter from Sir Clement Hill of British Foreign Office offering Uganda.

Aug. 22-28   Sixth Zionist Congress held at Basle. Uganda conflict.

1904—May 16   Last entry in Diaries—letter to Schiff.

July 3   Death of Theodor Herzl.

A CATALOG OF SELECTED
DOVER BOOKS
IN ALL FIELDS OF INTEREST

A CATALOG OF SELECTED DOVER
BOOKS IN ALL FIELDS OF INTEREST

CONCERNING THE SPIRITUAL IN ART, Wassily Kandinsky. Pioneering work by father of abstract art. Thoughts on color theory, nature of art. Analysis of earlier masters. 12 illustrations. 80pp. of text. 5⅜ x 8½. 0-486-23411-8

CELTIC ART: The Methods of Construction, George Bain. Simple geometric techniques for making Celtic interlacements, spirals, Kells-type initials, animals, humans, etc. Over 500 illustrations. 160pp. 9 x 12. (Available in U.S. only.) 0-486-22923-8

AN ATLAS OF ANATOMY FOR ARTISTS, Fritz Schider. Most thorough reference work on art anatomy in the world. Hundreds of illustrations, including selections from works by Vesalius, Leonardo, Goya, Ingres, Michelangelo, others. 593 illustrations. 192pp. 7⅛ x 10¼. 0-486-20241-0

CELTIC HAND STROKE-BY-STROKE (Irish Half-Uncial from "The Book of Kells"): An Arthur Baker Calligraphy Manual, Arthur Baker. Complete guide to creating each letter of the alphabet in distinctive Celtic manner. Covers hand position, strokes, pens, inks, paper, more. Illustrated. 48pp. 8¼ x 11. 0-486-24336-2

EASY ORIGAMI, John Montroll. Charming collection of 32 projects (hat, cup, pelican, piano, swan, many more) specially designed for the novice origami hobbyist. Clearly illustrated easy-to-follow instructions insure that even beginning papercrafters will achieve successful results. 48pp. 8¼ x 11. 0-486-27298-2

BLOOMINGDALE'S ILLUSTRATED 1886 CATALOG: Fashions, Dry Goods and Housewares, Bloomingdale Brothers. Famed merchants' extremely rare catalog depicting about 1,700 products: clothing, housewares, firearms, dry goods, jewelry, more. Invaluable for dating, identifying vintage items. Also, copyright-free graphics for artists, designers. Co-published with Henry Ford Museum & Greenfield Village. 160pp. 8¼ x 11. 0-486-25780-0

THE ART OF WORLDLY WISDOM, Baltasar Gracian. "Think with the few and speak with the many," "Friends are a second existence," and "Be able to forget" are among this 1637 volume's 300 pithy maxims. A perfect source of mental and spiritual refreshment, it can be opened at random and appreciated either in brief or at length. 128pp. 5⅜ x 8½. 0-486-44034-6

JOHNSON'S DICTIONARY: A Modern Selection, Samuel Johnson (E. L. McAdam and George Milne, eds.). This modern version reduces the original 1755 edition's 2,300 pages of definitions and literary examples to a more manageable length, retaining the verbal pleasure and historical curiosity of the original. 480pp. 5³⁄₁₆ x 8¼. 0-486-44089-3

ADVENTURES OF HUCKLEBERRY FINN, Mark Twain, Illustrated by E. W. Kemble. A work of eternal richness and complexity, a source of ongoing critical debate, and a literary landmark, Twain's 1885 masterpiece about a barefoot boy's journey of self-discovery has enthralled readers around the world. This handsome clothbound reproduction of the first edition features all 174 of the original black-and-white illustrations. 368pp. 5⅜ x 8½. 0-486-44322-1

STICKLEY CRAFTSMAN FURNITURE CATALOGS, Gustav Stickley and L. & J. G. Stickley. Beautiful, functional furniture in two authentic catalogs from 1910. 594 illustrations, including 277 photos, show settles, rockers, armchairs, reclining chairs, bookcases, desks, tables. 183pp. 6½ x 9¼.   0-486-23838-5

AMERICAN LOCOMOTIVES IN HISTORIC PHOTOGRAPHS: 1858 to 1949, Ron Ziel (ed.). A rare collection of 126 meticulously detailed official photographs, called "builder portraits," of American locomotives that majestically chronicle the rise of steam locomotive power in America. Introduction. Detailed captions. xi+ 129pp. 9 x 12.   0-486-27393-8

AMERICA'S LIGHTHOUSES: An Illustrated History, Francis Ross Holland, Jr. Delightfully written, profusely illustrated fact-filled survey of over 200 American light-houses since 1716. History, anecdotes, technological advances, more. 240pp. 8 x 10¾.
0-486-25576-X

TOWARDS A NEW ARCHITECTURE, Le Corbusier. Pioneering manifesto by founder of "International School." Technical and aesthetic theories, views of industry, economics, relation of form to function, "mass-production split" and much more. Profusely illustrated. 320pp. 6⅛ x 9¼. (Available in U.S. only.)   0-486-25023-7

HOW THE OTHER HALF LIVES, Jacob Riis. Famous journalistic record, expos-ing poverty and degradation of New York slums around 1900, by major social reformer. 100 striking and influential photographs. 233pp. 10 x 7⅞.   0-486-22012-5

FRUIT KEY AND TWIG KEY TO TREES AND SHRUBS, William M. Harlow. One of the handiest and most widely used identification aids. Fruit key covers 120 deciduous and evergreen species; twig key 160 deciduous species. Easily used. Over 300 photographs. 126pp. 5⅜ x 8½.   0-486-20511-8

COMMON BIRD SONGS, Dr. Donald J. Borror. Songs of 60 most common U.S. birds: robins, sparrows, cardinals, bluejays, finches, more–arranged in order of increasing complexity. Up to 9 variations of songs of each species.
Cassette and manual 0-486-99911-4

ORCHIDS AS HOUSE PLANTS, Rebecca Tyson Northen. Grow cattleyas and many other kinds of orchids–in a window, in a case, or under artificial light. 63 illustrations. 148pp. 5⅜ x 8½.   0-486-23261-1

MONSTER MAZES, Dave Phillips. Masterful mazes at four levels of difficulty. Avoid deadly perils and evil creatures to find magical treasures. Solutions for all 32 exciting illustrated puzzles. 48pp. 8¼ x 11.   0-486-26005-4

MOZART'S DON GIOVANNI (DOVER OPERA LIBRETTO SERIES), Wolfgang Amadeus Mozart. Introduced and translated by Ellen H. Bleiler. Standard Italian libretto, with complete English translation. Convenient and thoroughly portable–an ideal companion for reading along with a recording or the performance itself. Introduction. List of characters. Plot summary. 121pp. 5¼ x 8½.   0-486-24944-1

FRANK LLOYD WRIGHT'S DANA HOUSE, Donald Hoffmann. Pictorial essay of residential masterpiece with over 160 interior and exterior photos, plans, eleva-tions, sketches and studies. 128pp. 9¼ x 10¾.   0-486-29120-0

THE CLARINET AND CLARINET PLAYING, David Pino. Lively, comprehensive work features suggestions about technique, musicianship, and musical interpretation, as well as guidelines for teaching, making your own reeds, and preparing for public performance. Includes an intriguing look at clarinet history. "A godsend," *The Clarinet,* Journal of the International Clarinet Society. Appendixes. 7 illus. 320pp. 5⅜ x 8½. 0-486-40270-3

HOLLYWOOD GLAMOR PORTRAITS, John Kobal (ed.). 145 photos from 1926-49. Harlow, Gable, Bogart, Bacall; 94 stars in all. Full background on photographers, technical aspects. 160pp. 8⅜ x 11¼. 0-486-23352-9

THE RAVEN AND OTHER FAVORITE POEMS, Edgar Allan Poe. Over 40 of the author's most memorable poems: "The Bells," "Ulalume," "Israfel," "To Helen," "The Conqueror Worm," "Eldorado," "Annabel Lee," many more. Alphabetic lists of titles and first lines. 64pp. 5³⁄₁₆ x 8¼. 0-486-26685-0

PERSONAL MEMOIRS OF U. S. GRANT, Ulysses Simpson Grant. Intelligent, deeply moving firsthand account of Civil War campaigns, considered by many the finest military memoirs ever written. Includes letters, historic photographs, maps and more. 528pp. 6⅛ x 9¼. 0-486-28587-1

POE ILLUSTRATED: Art by Doré, Dulac, Rackham and Others, selected and edited by Jeff A. Menges. More than 100 compelling illustrations, in brilliant color and crisp black-and-white, include scenes from "The Raven," "The Pit and the Pendulum," "The Gold-Bug," and other stories and poems. 96pp. 8⅜ x 11.

0-486-45746-X

RUSSIAN STORIES/RUSSKIE RASSKAZY: A Dual-Language Book, edited by Gleb Struve. Twelve tales by such masters as Chekhov, Tolstoy, Dostoevsky, Pushkin, others. Excellent word-for-word English translations on facing pages, plus teaching and study aids, Russian/English vocabulary, biographical/critical introductions, more. 416pp. 5⅜ x 8½. 0-486-26244-8

PHILADELPHIA THEN AND NOW: 60 Sites Photographed in the Past and Present, Kenneth Finkel and Susan Oyama. Rare photographs of City Hall, Logan Square, Independence Hall, Betsy Ross House, other landmarks juxtaposed with contemporary views. Captures changing face of historic city. Introduction. Captions. 128pp. 8¼ x 11. 0-486-25790-8

NORTH AMERICAN INDIAN LIFE: Customs and Traditions of 23 Tribes, Elsie Clews Parsons (ed.). 27 fictionalized essays by noted anthropologists examine religion, customs, government, additional facets of life among the Winnebago, Crow, Zuni, Eskimo, other tribes. 480pp. 6⅛ x 9¼. 0-486-27377-6

TECHNICAL MANUAL AND DICTIONARY OF CLASSICAL BALLET, Gail Grant. Defines, explains, comments on steps, movements, poses and concepts. 15-page pictorial section. Basic book for student, viewer. 127pp. 5⅜ x 8½.

0-486-21843-0

THE MALE AND FEMALE FIGURE IN MOTION: 60 Classic Photographic Sequences, Eadweard Muybridge. 60 true-action photographs of men and women walking, running, climbing, bending, turning, etc., reproduced from a rare 19th-century masterpiece. vi + 121pp. 9 x 12. 0-486-24745-7

ANIMALS: 1,419 Copyright-Free Illustrations of Mammals, Birds, Fish, Insects, etc., Jim Harter (ed.). Clear wood engravings present, in extremely lifelike poses, over 1,000 species of animals. One of the most extensive pictorial sourcebooks of its kind. Captions. Index. 284pp. 9 x 12. 0-486-23766-4

1001 QUESTIONS ANSWERED ABOUT THE SEASHORE, N. J. Berrill and Jacquelyn Berrill. Queries answered about dolphins, sea snails, sponges, starfish, fishes, shore birds, many others. Covers appearance, breeding, growth, feeding, much more. 305pp. 5¼ x 8¼. 0-486-23366-9

ATTRACTING BIRDS TO YOUR YARD, William J. Weber. Easy-to-follow guide offers advice on how to attract the greatest diversity of birds: birdhouses, feeders, water and waterers, much more. 96pp. 5³/₁₆ x 8¼. 0-486-28927-3

MEDICINAL AND OTHER USES OF NORTH AMERICAN PLANTS: A Historical Survey with Special Reference to the Eastern Indian Tribes, Charlotte Erichsen-Brown. Chronological historical citations document 500 years of usage of plants, trees, shrubs native to eastern Canada, northeastern U.S. Also complete identifying information. 343 illustrations. 544pp. 6½ x 9¼. 0-486-25951-X

STORYBOOK MAZES, Dave Phillips. 23 stories and mazes on two-page spreads: Wizard of Oz, Treasure Island, Robin Hood, etc. Solutions. 64pp. 8¼ x 11. 0-486-23628-5

AMERICAN NEGRO SONGS: 230 Folk Songs and Spirituals, Religious and Secular, John W. Work. This authoritative study traces the African influences of songs sung and played by black Americans at work, in church, and as entertainment. The author discusses the lyric significance of such songs as "Swing Low, Sweet Chariot," "John Henry," and others and offers the words and music for 230 songs. Bibliography. Index of Song Titles. 272pp. 6½ x 9¼. 0-486-40271-1

MOVIE-STAR PORTRAITS OF THE FORTIES, John Kobal (ed.). 163 glamor, studio photos of 106 stars of the 1940s: Rita Hayworth, Ava Gardner, Marlon Brando, Clark Gable, many more. 176pp. 8⅜ x 11¼. 0-486-23546-7

YEKL and THE IMPORTED BRIDEGROOM AND OTHER STORIES OF YIDDISH NEW YORK, Abraham Cahan. Film Hester Street based on *Yekl* (1896). Novel, other stories among first about Jewish immigrants on N.Y.'s East Side. 240pp. 5⅜ x 8½. 0-486-22427-9

SELECTED POEMS, Walt Whitman. Generous sampling from *Leaves of Grass.* Twenty-four poems include "I Hear America Singing," "Song of the Open Road," "I Sing the Body Electric," "When Lilacs Last in the Dooryard Bloom'd," "O Captain! My Captain!"—all reprinted from an authoritative edition. Lists of titles and first lines. 128pp. 5³/₁₆ x 8¼. 0-486-26878-0

SONGS OF EXPERIENCE: Facsimile Reproduction with 26 Plates in Full Color, William Blake. 26 full-color plates from a rare 1826 edition. Includes "The Tyger," "London," "Holy Thursday," and other poems. Printed text of poems. 48pp. 5¼ x 7. 0-486-24636-1

THE BEST TALES OF HOFFMANN, E. T. A. Hoffmann. 10 of Hoffmann's most important stories: "Nutcracker and the King of Mice," "The Golden Flowerpot," etc. 458pp. 5⅜ x 8½. 0-486-21793-0

THE BOOK OF TEA, Kakuzo Okakura. Minor classic of the Orient: entertaining, charming explanation, interpretation of traditional Japanese culture in terms of tea ceremony. 94pp. 5⅜ x 8½. 0-486-20070-1

CATALOG OF DOVER BOOKS

FRENCH STORIES/CONTES FRANÇAIS: A Dual-Language Book, Wallace Fowlie. Ten stories by French masters, Voltaire to Camus: "Micromegas" by Voltaire; "The Atheist's Mass" by Balzac; "Minuet" by de Maupassant; "The Guest" by Camus, six more. Excellent English translations on facing pages. Also French-English vocabulary list, exercises, more. 352pp. 5⅜ x 8½. 0-486-26443-2

CHICAGO AT THE TURN OF THE CENTURY IN PHOTOGRAPHS: 122 Historic Views from the Collections of the Chicago Historical Society, Larry A. Viskochil. Rare large-format prints offer detailed views of City Hall, State Street, the Loop, Hull House, Union Station, many other landmarks, circa 1904-1913. Introduction. Captions. Maps. 144pp. 9⅜ x 12¼. 0-486-24656-6

OLD BROOKLYN IN EARLY PHOTOGRAPHS, 1865-1929, William Lee Younger. Luna Park, Gravesend race track, construction of Grand Army Plaza, moving of Hotel Brighton, etc. 157 previously unpublished photographs. 165pp. 8⅞ x 11¾.
0-486-23587-4

THE MYTHS OF THE NORTH AMERICAN INDIANS, Lewis Spence. Rich anthology of the myths and legends of the Algonquins, Iroquois, Pawnees and Sioux, prefaced by an extensive historical and ethnological commentary. 36 illustrations. 480pp. 5⅜ x 8½. 0-486-25967-6

AN ENCYCLOPEDIA OF BATTLES: Accounts of Over 1,560 Battles from 1479 B.C. to the Present, David Eggenberger. Essential details of every major battle in recorded history from the first battle of Megiddo in 1479 B.C. to Grenada in 1984. List of Battle Maps. New Appendix covering the years 1967-1984. Index. 99 illustrations. 544pp. 6½ x 9¼. 0-486-24913-1

SAILING ALONE AROUND THE WORLD, Captain Joshua Slocum. First man to sail around the world, alone, in small boat. One of the great feats of seamanship told in delightful manner. 67 illustrations. 294pp. 5⅜ x 8½. 0-486-20326-3

ANARCHISM AND OTHER ESSAYS, Emma Goldman. Powerful, penetrating, prophetic essays on direct action, role of minorities, prison reform, puritan hypocrisy, violence, etc. 271pp. 5⅜ x 8½. 0-486-22484-8

MYTHS OF THE HINDUS AND BUDDHISTS, Ananda K. Coomaraswamy and Sister Nivedita. Great stories of the epics; deeds of Krishna, Shiva, taken from puranas, Vedas, folk tales; etc. 32 illustrations. 400pp. 5⅜ x 8½. 0-486-21759-0

MY BONDAGE AND MY FREEDOM, Frederick Douglass. Born a slave, Douglass became outspoken force in antislavery movement. The best of Douglass' autobiographies. Graphic description of slave life. 464pp. 5⅜ x 8½. 0-486-22457-0

FOLLOWING THE EQUATOR: A Journey Around the World, Mark Twain. Fascinating humorous account of 1897 voyage to Hawaii, Australia, India, New Zealand, etc. Ironic, bemused reports on peoples, customs, climate, flora and fauna, politics, much more. 197 illustrations. 720pp. 5⅜ x 8½. 0-486-26113-1

GREAT SPEECHES BY AMERICAN WOMEN, edited by James Daley. Here are 21 legendary speeches from the country's most inspirational female voices, including Sojourner Truth, Susan B. Anthony, Eleanor Roosevelt, Hillary Rodham Clinton, Nancy Pelosi, and many others. 192pp. 5³⁄₁₆ x 8¼. 0-486-46141-6

THE MYTHS OF GREECE AND ROME, H. A. Guerber. A classic of mythology, generously illustrated, long prized for its simple, graphic, accurate retelling of the principal myths of Greece and Rome, and for its commentary on their origins and significance. With 64 illustrations by Michelangelo, Raphael, Titian, Rubens, Canova, Bernini and others. 480pp. 5⅜ x 8½. 0-486-27584-1

PSYCHOLOGY OF MUSIC, Carl E. Seashore. Classic work discusses music as a medium from psychological viewpoint. Clear treatment of physical acoustics, auditory apparatus, sound perception, development of musical skills, nature of musical feeling, host of other topics. 88 figures. 408pp. 5⅜ x 8½. 0-486-21851-1

LIFE IN ANCIENT EGYPT, Adolf Erman. Fullest, most thorough, detailed older account with much not in more recent books, domestic life, religion, magic, medicine, commerce, much more. Many illustrations reproduce tomb paintings, carvings, hieroglyphs, etc. 597pp. 5⅜ x 8½. 0-486-22632-8

SUNDIALS, Their Theory and Construction, Albert Waugh. Far and away the best, most thorough coverage of ideas, mathematics concerned, types, construction, adjusting anywhere. Simple, nontechnical treatment allows even children to build several of these dials. Over 100 illustrations. 230pp. 5⅜ x 8½. 0-486-22947-5

GREAT SPEECHES BY AFRICAN AMERICANS: Frederick Douglass, Sojourner Truth, Dr. Martin Luther King, Jr., Barack Obama, and Others, edited by James Daley. Tracing the struggle for freedom and civil rights across two centuries, this anthology comprises speeches by Martin Luther King, Jr., Marcus Garvey, Malcolm X, Barack Obama, and many other influential figures. 160pp. 5³⁄₁₆ x 8¼.
0-486-44761-8

OLD-TIME VIGNETTES IN FULL COLOR, Carol Belanger Grafton (ed.). Over 390 charming, often sentimental illustrations, selected from archives of Victorian graphics—pretty women posing, children playing, food, flowers, kittens and puppies, smiling cherubs, birds and butterflies, much more. All copyright-free. 48pp. 9¼ x 12¼.
0-486-27269-9

PERSPECTIVE FOR ARTISTS, Rex Vicat Cole. Depth, perspective of sky and sea, shadows, much more, not usually covered. 391 diagrams, 81 reproductions of drawings and paintings. 279pp. 5⅜ x 8½. 0-486-22487-2

DRAWING THE LIVING FIGURE, Joseph Sheppard. Innovative approach to artistic anatomy focuses on specifics of surface anatomy, rather than muscles and bones. Over 170 drawings of live models in front, back and side views, and in widely varying poses. Accompanying diagrams. 177 illustrations. Introduction. Index. 144pp. 8⅜ x11¼. 0-486-26723-7

GOTHIC AND OLD ENGLISH ALPHABETS: 100 Complete Fonts, Dan X. Solo. Add power, elegance to posters, signs, other graphics with 100 stunning copyright-free alphabets: Blackstone, Dolbey, Germania, 97 more—including many lower-case, numerals, punctuation marks. 104pp. 8⅛ x 11. 0-486-24695-7

THE BOOK OF WOOD CARVING, Charles Marshall Sayers. Finest book for beginners discusses fundamentals and offers 34 designs. "Absolutely first rate . . . well thought out and well executed."–E. J. Tangerman. 118pp. 7¾ x 10⅝. 0-486-23654-4

ILLUSTRATED CATALOG OF CIVIL WAR MILITARY GOODS: Union Army Weapons, Insignia, Uniform Accessories, and Other Equipment, Schuyler, Hartley, and Graham. Rare, profusely illustrated 1846 catalog includes Union Army uniform and dress regulations, arms and ammunition, coats, insignia, flags, swords, rifles, etc. 226 illustrations. 160pp. 9 x 12. 0-486-24939-5

WOMEN'S FASHIONS OF THE EARLY 1900s: An Unabridged Republication of "New York Fashions, 1909," National Cloak & Suit Co. Rare catalog of mail-order fashions documents women's and children's clothing styles shortly after the turn of the century. Captions offer full descriptions, prices. Invaluable resource for fashion, costume historians. Approximately 725 illustrations. 128pp. 8⅜ x 11¼. 0-486-27276-1

CATALOG OF DOVER BOOKS

HOW TO DO BEADWORK, Mary White. Fundamental book on craft from simple projects to five-bead chains and woven works. 106 illustrations. 142pp. 5⅜ x 8.
0-486-20697-1

THE 1912 AND 1915 GUSTAV STICKLEY FURNITURE CATALOGS, Gustav Stickley. With over 200 detailed illustrations and descriptions, these two catalogs are essential reading and reference materials and identification guides for Stickley furniture. Captions cite materials, dimensions and prices. 112pp. 6½ x 9¼. 0-486-26676-1

SIX GREAT DIALOGUES: Apology, Crito, Phaedo, Phaedrus, Symposium, The Republic, Plato, translated by Benjamin Jowett. Plato's Dialogues rank among Western civilization's most important and influential philosophical works. These 6 selections of his major works explore a broad range of enduringly relevant issues. Authoritative Jowett translations. 480pp. 5³⁄₁₆ x 8¼. 0-486-45465-7

DEMONOLATRY: An Account of the Historical Practice of Witchcraft, Nicolas Remy, edited with an Introduction and Notes by Montague Summers, translated by E. A. Ashwin. This extremely influential 1595 study was frequently cited at witchcraft trials. In addition to lurid details of satanic pacts and sexual perversity, it presents the particulars of numerous court cases. 240pp. 6½ x 9¼. 0-486-46137-8

VICTORIAN FASHIONS AND COSTUMES FROM HARPER'S BAZAAR, 1867–1898, Stella Blum (ed.). Day costumes, evening wear, sports clothes, shoes, hats, other accessories in over 1,000 detailed engravings. 320pp. 9⅜ x 12¼.
0-486-22990-4

THE LONG ISLAND RAIL ROAD IN EARLY PHOTOGRAPHS, Ron Ziel. Over 220 rare photos, informative text document origin (1844) and development of rail service on Long Island. Vintage views of early trains, locomotives, stations, passengers, crews, much more. Captions. 8⅞ x 11¾. 0-486-26301-0

VOYAGE OF THE LIBERDADE, Joshua Slocum. Great 19th-century mariner's thrilling, first-hand account of the wreck of his ship off South America, the 35-foot boat he built from the wreckage, and its remarkable voyage home. 128pp. 5⅜ x 8½.
0-486-40022-0

TEN BOOKS ON ARCHITECTURE, Vitruvius. The most important book ever written on architecture. Early Roman aesthetics, technology, classical orders, site selection, all other aspects. Morgan translation. 331pp. 5⅜ x 8½. 0-486-20645-9

THE HUMAN FIGURE IN MOTION, Eadweard Muybridge. More than 4,500 stopped-action photos, in action series, showing undraped men, women, children jumping, lying down, throwing, sitting, wrestling, carrying, etc. 390pp. 7⅞ x 10⅝.
0-486-20204-6 Clothbd.

TREES OF THE EASTERN AND CENTRAL UNITED STATES AND CANADA, William M. Harlow. Best one-volume guide to 140 trees. Full descriptions, woodlore, range, etc. Over 600 illustrations. Handy size. 288pp. 4½ x 6⅜. 0-486-20395-6

MY FIRST BOOK OF TCHAIKOVSKY: Favorite Pieces in Easy Piano Arrangements, edited by David Dutkanicz. These special arrangements of favorite Tchaikovsky themes are ideal for beginner pianists, child or adult. Contents include themes from "The Nutcracker," "March Slav," Symphonies Nos. 5 and 6, "Swan Lake," "Sleeping Beauty," and more. 48pp. 8¼ x 11. 0-486-46416-4

BIG BOOK OF MAZES AND LABYRINTHS, Walter Shepherd. 50 mazes and labyrinths in all—classical, solid, ripple, and more—in one great volume. Perfect inexpensive puzzler for clever youngsters. Full solutions. 112pp. 8⅛ x 11. 0-486-22951-3

PIANO TUNING, J. Cree Fischer. Clearest, best book for beginner, amateur. Simple repairs, raising dropped notes, tuning by easy method of flattened fifths. No previous skills needed. 4 illustrations. 201pp. 5⅜ x 8½. 0-486-23267-0

HINTS TO SINGERS, Lillian Nordica. Selecting the right teacher, developing confidence, overcoming stage fright, and many other important skills receive thoughtful discussion in this indispensible guide, written by a world-famous diva of four decades' experience. 96pp. 5⅜ x 8½. 0-486-40094-8

THE COMPLETE NONSENSE OF EDWARD LEAR, Edward Lear. All nonsense limericks, zany alphabets, Owl and Pussycat, songs, nonsense botany, etc., illustrated by Lear. Total of 320pp. 5⅜ x 8½. (Available in U.S. only.) 0-486-20167-8

VICTORIAN PARLOUR POETRY: An Annotated Anthology, Michael R. Turner. 117 gems by Longfellow, Tennyson, Browning, many lesser-known poets. "The Village Blacksmith," "Curfew Must Not Ring Tonight," "Only a Baby Small," dozens more, often difficult to find elsewhere. Index of poets, titles, first lines. xxiii + 325pp. 5⅝ x 8¼. 0-486-27044-0

DUBLINERS, James Joyce. Fifteen stories offer vivid, tightly focused observations of the lives of Dublin's poorer classes. At least one, "The Dead," is considered a masterpiece. Reprinted complete and unabridged from standard edition. 160pp. 5³/₁₆ x 8¼.
0-486-26870-5

THE LITTLE RED SCHOOLHOUSE, Eric Sloane. Harkening back to a time when the three Rs stood for reading, 'riting, and religion, Sloane's sketchbook explores the history of early American schools. Includes marvelous illustrations of one-room New England schoolhouses, desks, and benches. 48pp. 8¼ x 11. 0-486-45604-8

THE BOOK OF THE SACRED MAGIC OF ABRAMELIN THE MAGE, translated by S. MacGregor Mathers. Medieval manuscript of ceremonial magic. Basic document in Aleister Crowley, Golden Dawn groups. 268pp. 5⅜ x 8½.
0-486-23211-5

THE BATTLES THAT CHANGED HISTORY, Fletcher Pratt. Eminent historian profiles 16 crucial conflicts, ancient to modern, that changed the course of civilization. 352pp. 5⅜ x 8½. 0-486-41129-X

NEW RUSSIAN-ENGLISH AND ENGLISH-RUSSIAN DICTIONARY, M. A. O'Brien. This is a remarkably handy Russian dictionary, containing a surprising amount of information, including over 70,000 entries. 366pp. 4½ x 6⅛.
0-486-20208-9

NEW YORK IN THE FORTIES, Andreas Feininger. 162 brilliant photographs by the well-known photographer, formerly with *Life* magazine. Commuters, shoppers, Times Square at night, much else from city at its peak. Captions by John von Hartz. 181pp. 9¼ x 10¾. 0-486-23585-8

INDIAN SIGN LANGUAGE, William Tomkins. Over 525 signs developed by Sioux and other tribes. Written instructions and diagrams. Also 290 pictographs. 111pp. 6⅛ x 9¼. 0-486-22029-X

ANATOMY: A Complete Guide for Artists, Joseph Sheppard. A master of figure drawing shows artists how to render human anatomy convincingly. Over 460 illustrations. 224pp. 8⅜ x 11¼. 0-486-27279-6

MEDIEVAL CALLIGRAPHY: Its History and Technique, Marc Drogin. Spirited history, comprehensive instruction manual covers 13 styles (ca. 4th century through 15th). Excellent photographs; directions for duplicating medieval techniques with modern tools. 224pp. 8⅜ x 11¼. 0-486-26142-5

CATALOG OF DOVER BOOKS

DRIED FLOWERS: How to Prepare Them, Sarah Whitlock and Martha Rankin. Complete instructions on how to use silica gel, meal and borax, perlite aggregate, sand and borax, glycerine and water to create attractive permanent flower arrangements. 12 illustrations. 32pp. 5⅜ x 8½.   0-486-21802-3

EASY-TO-MAKE BIRD FEEDERS FOR WOODWORKERS, Scott D. Campbell. Detailed, simple-to-use guide for designing, constructing, caring for and using feeders. Text, illustrations for 12 classic and contemporary designs. 96pp. 5⅜ x 8½.
0-486-25847-5

THE COMPLETE BOOK OF BIRDHOUSE CONSTRUCTION FOR WOOD-WORKERS, Scott D. Campbell. Detailed instructions, illustrations, tables. Also data on bird habitat and instinct patterns. Bibliography. 3 tables. 63 illustrations in 15 figures. 48pp. 5¼ x 8½.   0-486-24407-5

SCOTTISH WONDER TALES FROM MYTH AND LEGEND, Donald A. Mackenzie. 16 lively tales tell of giants rumbling down mountainsides, of a magic wand that turns stone pillars into warriors, of gods and goddesses, evil hags, powerful forces and more. 240pp. 5⅜ x 8½.   0-486-29677-6

THE HISTORY OF UNDERCLOTHES, C. Willett Cunnington and Phyllis Cunnington. Fascinating, well-documented survey covering six centuries of English undergarments, enhanced with over 100 illustrations: 12th-century laced-up bodice, footed long drawers (1795), 19th-century bustles, l9th-century corsets for men, Victorian "bust improvers," much more. 272pp. 5⅜ x 8¼.   0-486-27124-2

FIRST FRENCH READER: A Beginner's Dual-Language Book, edited and translated by Stanley Appelbaum. This anthology introduces fifty legendary writers—Voltaire, Balzac, Baudelaire, Proust, more—through passages from The Red and the Black, Les Misérables, Madame Bovary, and other classics. Original French text plus English translation on facing pages. 240pp. 5⅜ x 8½.   0-486-46178-5

WILBUR AND ORVILLE: A Biography of the Wright Brothers, Fred Howard. Definitive, crisply written study tells the full story of the brothers' lives and work. A vividly written biography, unparalleled in scope and color, that also captures the spirit of an extraordinary era. 560pp. 6⅛ x 9¼.   0-486-40297-5

THE ARTS OF THE SAILOR: Knotting, Splicing and Ropework, Hervey Garrett Smith. Indispensable shipboard reference covers tools, basic knots and useful hitches; handsewing and canvas work, more. Over 100 illustrations. Delightful reading for sea lovers. 256pp. 5⅜ x 8½.   0-486-26440-8

FRANK LLOYD WRIGHT'S FALLINGWATER: The House and Its History, Second, Revised Edition, Donald Hoffmann. A total revision—both in text and illustrations—of the standard document on Fallingwater, the boldest, most personal architectural statement of Wright's mature years, updated with valuable new material from the recently opened Frank Lloyd Wright Archives. "Fascinating"—The New York Times. 116 illustrations. 128pp. 9¼ x 10¾.   0-486-27430-6

PHOTOGRAPHIC SKETCHBOOK OF THE CIVIL WAR, Alexander Gardner. 100 photos taken on field during the Civil War. Famous shots of Manassas Harper's Ferry, Lincoln, Richmond, slave pens, etc. 244pp. 10⅝ x 8¼.   0-486-22731-6

FIVE ACRES AND INDEPENDENCE, Maurice G. Kains. Great back-to-the-land classic explains basics of self-sufficient farming. The one book to get. 95 illustrations. 397pp. 5⅜ x 8½.   0-486-20974-1

A MODERN HERBAL, Margaret Grieve. Much the fullest, most exact, most useful compilation of herbal material. Gigantic alphabetical encyclopedia, from aconite to zedoary, gives botanical information, medical properties, folklore, economic uses, much else. Indispensable to serious reader. 161 illustrations. 888pp. 6½ x 9¼. 2-vol. set. (Available in U.S. only.)　　　Vol. I: 0-486-22798-7　　Vol. II: 0-486-22799-5

HIDDEN TREASURE MAZE BOOK, Dave Phillips. Solve 34 challenging mazes accompanied by heroic tales of adventure. Evil dragons, people-eating plants, blood-thirsty giants, many more dangerous adversaries lurk at every twist and turn. 34 mazes, stories, solutions. 48pp. 8¼ x 11.　　　　　　　　　　　0-486-24566-7

LETTERS OF W. A. MOZART, Wolfgang A. Mozart. Remarkable letters show bawdy wit, humor, imagination, musical insights, contemporary musical world; includes some letters from Leopold Mozart. 276pp. 5⅜ x 8½.　　　0-486-22859-2

BASIC PRINCIPLES OF CLASSICAL BALLET, Agrippina Vaganova. Great Russian theoretician, teacher explains methods for teaching classical ballet. 118 illustrations. 175pp. 5⅜ x 8½.　　　　　　　　　　　　　　　0-486-22036-2

THE JUMPING FROG, Mark Twain. Revenge edition. The original story of The Celebrated Jumping Frog of Calaveras County, a hapless French translation, and Twain's hilarious "retranslation" from the French. 12 illustrations. 66pp. 5⅜ x 8½.
　　　　　　　　　　　　　　　　　　　　　　　　　　0-486-22686-7

BEST REMEMBERED POEMS, Martin Gardner (ed.). The 126 poems in this superb collection of 19th- and 20th-century British and American verse range from Shelley's "To a Skylark" to the impassioned "Renascence" of Edna St. Vincent Millay and to Edward Lear's whimsical "The Owl and the Pussycat." 224pp. 5⅜ x 8½.
　　　　　　　　　　　　　　　　　　　　　　　　　　0-486-27165-X

COMPLETE SONNETS, William Shakespeare. Over 150 exquisite poems deal with love, friendship, the tyranny of time, beauty's evanescence, death and other themes in language of remarkable power, precision and beauty. Glossary of archaic terms. 80pp. 5³⁄₁₆ x 8¼.　　　　　　　　　　　　　　　　　　0-486-26686-9

HISTORIC HOMES OF THE AMERICAN PRESIDENTS, Second, Revised Edition, Irvin Haas. A traveler's guide to American Presidential homes, most open to the public, depicting and describing homes occupied by every American President from George Washington to George Bush. With visiting hours, admission charges, travel routes. 175 photographs. Index. 160pp. 8¼ x 11.　　　0-486-26751-2

THE WIT AND HUMOR OF OSCAR WILDE, Alvin Redman (ed.). More than 1,000 ripostes, paradoxes, wisecracks: Work is the curse of the drinking classes; I can resist everything except temptation; etc. 258pp. 5⅜ x 8½.　　　0-486-20602-5

SHAKESPEARE LEXICON AND QUOTATION DICTIONARY, Alexander Schmidt. Full definitions, locations, shades of meaning in every word in plays and poems. More than 50,000 exact quotations. 1,485pp. 6½ x 9¼. 2-vol. set.
　　　　　　　　　Vol. 1: 0-486-22726-X　　　Vol. 2: 0-486-22727-8

SELECTED POEMS, Emily Dickinson. Over 100 best-known, best-loved poems by one of America's foremost poets, reprinted from authoritative early editions. No comparable edition at this price. Index of first lines. 64pp. 5³⁄₁₆ x 8¼. 0-486-26466-1

THE INSIDIOUS DR. FU-MANCHU, Sax Rohmer. The first of the popular mystery series introduces a pair of English detectives to their archnemesis, the diabolical Dr. Fu-Manchu. Flavorful atmosphere, fast-paced action, and colorful characters enliven this classic of the genre. 208pp. 5³⁄₁₆ x 8¼.　　　　　0-486-29898-1

CATALOG OF DOVER BOOKS

THE MALLEUS MALEFICARUM OF KRAMER AND SPRENGER, translated by Montague Summers. Full text of most important witchhunter's "bible," used by both Catholics and Protestants. 278pp. 6⅝ x 10. 0-486-22802-9

SPANISH STORIES/CUENTOS ESPAÑOLES: A Dual-Language Book, Angel Flores (ed.). Unique format offers 13 great stories in Spanish by Cervantes, Borges, others. Faithful English translations on facing pages. 352pp. 5⅜ x 8½.
0-486-25399-6

GARDEN CITY, LONG ISLAND, IN EARLY PHOTOGRAPHS, 1869–1919, Mildred H. Smith. Handsome treasury of 118 vintage pictures, accompanied by carefully researched captions, document the Garden City Hotel fire (1899), the Vanderbilt Cup Race (1908), the first airmail flight departing from the Nassau Boulevard Aerodrome (1911), and much more. 96pp. 8⅞ x 11¾. 0-486-40669-5

OLD QUEENS, N.Y., IN EARLY PHOTOGRAPHS, Vincent F. Seyfried and William Asadorian. Over 160 rare photographs of Maspeth, Jamaica, Jackson Heights, and other areas. Vintage views of DeWitt Clinton mansion, 1939 World's Fair and more. Captions. 192pp. 8⅞ x 11. 0-486-26358-4

CAPTURED BY THE INDIANS: 15 Firsthand Accounts, 1750-1870, Frederick Drimmer. Astounding true historical accounts of grisly torture, bloody conflicts, relentless pursuits, miraculous escapes and more, by people who lived to tell the tale. 384pp. 5⅜ x 8½. 0-486-24901-8

THE WORLD'S GREAT SPEECHES (Fourth Enlarged Edition), Lewis Copeland, Lawrence W. Lamm, and Stephen J. McKenna. Nearly 300 speeches provide public speakers with a wealth of updated quotes and inspiration—from Pericles' funeral oration and William Jennings Bryan's "Cross of Gold Speech" to Malcolm X's powerful words on the Black Revolution and Earl of Spenser's tribute to his sister, Diana, Princess of Wales. 944pp. 5⅜ x 8⅜. 0-486-40903-1

THE BOOK OF THE SWORD, Sir Richard F. Burton. Great Victorian scholar/adventurer's eloquent, erudite history of the "queen of weapons"—from prehistory to early Roman Empire. Evolution and development of early swords, variations (sabre, broadsword, cutlass, scimitar, etc.), much more. 336pp. 6⅛ x 9¼.
0-486-25434-8

AUTOBIOGRAPHY: The Story of My Experiments with Truth, Mohandas K. Gandhi. Boyhood, legal studies, purification, the growth of the Satyagraha (nonviolent protest) movement. Critical, inspiring work of the man responsible for the freedom of India. 480pp. 5⅜ x 8½. (Available in U.S. only.) 0-486-24593-4

CELTIC MYTHS AND LEGENDS, T. W. Rolleston. Masterful retelling of Irish and Welsh stories and tales. Cuchulain, King Arthur, Deirdre, the Grail, many more. First paperback edition. 58 full-page illustrations. 512pp. 5⅜ x 8½. 0-486-26507-2

THE PRINCIPLES OF PSYCHOLOGY, William James. Famous long course complete, unabridged. Stream of thought, time perception, memory, experimental methods; great work decades ahead of its time. 94 figures. 1,391pp. 5⅜ x 8½. 2-vol. set.
Vol. I: 0-486-20381-6   Vol. II: 0-486-20382-4

THE WORLD AS WILL AND REPRESENTATION, Arthur Schopenhauer. Definitive English translation of Schopenhauer's life work, correcting more than 1,000 errors, omissions in earlier translations. Translated by E. F. J. Payne. Total of 1,269pp. 5⅜ x 8½. 2-vol. set.   Vol. 1: 0-486-21761-2   Vol. 2: 0-486-21762-0

MAGIC AND MYSTERY IN TIBET, Madame Alexandra David-Neel. Experiences among lamas, magicians, sages, sorcerers, Bonpa wizards. A true psychic discovery. 32 illustrations. 321pp. 5⅜ x 8½. (Available in U.S. only.) 0-486-22682-4

THE EGYPTIAN BOOK OF THE DEAD, E. A. Wallis Budge. Complete reproduction of Ani's papyrus, finest ever found. Full hieroglyphic text, interlinear transliteration, word-for-word translation, smooth translation. 533pp. 6½ x 9¼.

0-486-21866-X

HISTORIC COSTUME IN PICTURES, Braun & Schneider. Over 1,450 costumed figures in clearly detailed engravings–from dawn of civilization to end of 19th century. Captions. Many folk costumes. 256pp. 8⅜ x 11¾. 0-486-23150-X

MATHEMATICS FOR THE NONMATHEMATICIAN, Morris Kline. Detailed, college-level treatment of mathematics in cultural and historical context, with numerous exercises. Recommended Reading Lists. Tables. Numerous figures. 641pp. 5⅜ x 8½. 0-486-24823-2

PROBABILISTIC METHODS IN THE THEORY OF STRUCTURES, Isaac Elishakoff. Well-written introduction covers the elements of the theory of probability from two or more random variables, the reliability of such multivariable structures, the theory of random function, Monte Carlo methods of treating problems incapable of exact solution, and more. Examples. 502pp. 5⅜ x 8½. 0-486-40691-1

THE RIME OF THE ANCIENT MARINER, Gustave Doré, S. T. Coleridge. Doré's finest work; 34 plates capture moods, subtleties of poem. Flawless full-size reproductions printed on facing pages with authoritative text of poem. "Beautiful. Simply beautiful."–*Publisher's Weekly.* 77pp. 9¼ x 12. 0-486-22305-1

SCULPTURE: Principles and Practice, Louis Slobodkin. Step-by-step approach to clay, plaster, metals, stone; classical and modern. 253 drawings, photos. 255pp. 8⅛ x 11. 0-486-22960-2

THE INFLUENCE OF SEA POWER UPON HISTORY, 1660–1783, A. T. Mahan. Influential classic of naval history and tactics still used as text in war colleges. First paperback edition. 4 maps. 24 battle plans. 640pp. 5⅜ x 8½. 0-486-25509-3

THE STORY OF THE TITANIC AS TOLD BY ITS SURVIVORS, Jack Winocour (ed.). What it was really like. Panic, despair, shocking inefficiency, and a little heroism. More thrilling than any fictional account. 26 illustrations. 320pp. 5⅜ x 8½.

0-486-20610-6

ONE TWO THREE . . . INFINITY: Facts and Speculations of Science, George Gamow. Great physicist's fascinating, readable overview of contemporary science: number theory, relativity, fourth dimension, entropy, genes, atomic structure, much more. 128 illustrations. Index. 352pp. 5⅜ x 8½. 0-486-25664-2

DALÍ ON MODERN ART: The Cuckolds of Antiquated Modern Art, Salvador Dalí. Influential painter skewers modern art and its practitioners. Outrageous evaluations of Picasso, Cézanne, Turner, more. 15 renderings of paintings discussed. 44 calligraphic decorations by Dalí. 96pp. 5⅜ x 8½. (Available in U.S. only.) 0-486-29220-7

ANTIQUE PLAYING CARDS: A Pictorial History, Henry René D'Allemagne. Over 900 elaborate, decorative images from rare playing cards (14th–20th centuries): Bacchus, death, dancing dogs, hunting scenes, royal coats of arms, players cheating, much more. 96pp. 9¼ x 12¼. 0-486-29265-7

MAKING FURNITURE MASTERPIECES: 30 Projects with Measured Drawings, Franklin H. Gottshall. Step-by-step instructions, illustrations for constructing handsome, useful pieces, among them a Sheraton desk, Chippendale chair, Spanish desk, Queen Anne table and a William and Mary dressing mirror. 224pp. 8⅛ x 11¼.
0-486-29338-6

NORTH AMERICAN INDIAN DESIGNS FOR ARTISTS AND CRAFTSPEOPLE, Eva Wilson. Over 360 authentic copyright-free designs adapted from Navajo blankets, Hopi pottery, Sioux buffalo hides, more. Geometrics, symbolic figures, plant and animal motifs, etc. 128pp. 8⅜ x 11. (Not for sale in the United Kingdom.) 0-486-25341-4

THE FOSSIL BOOK: A Record of Prehistoric Life, Patricia V. Rich et al. Profusely illustrated definitive guide covers everything from single-celled organisms and dinosaurs to birds and mammals and the interplay between climate and man. Over 1,500 illustrations. 760pp. 7½ x 10⅛. 0-486-29371-8

VICTORIAN ARCHITECTURAL DETAILS: Designs for Over 700 Stairs, Mantels, Doors, Windows, Cornices, Porches, and Other Decorative Elements, A. J. Bicknell & Company. Everything from dormer windows and piazzas to balconies and gable ornaments. Also includes elevations and floor plans for handsome, private residences and commercial structures. 80pp. 9⅜ x 12¼. 0-486-44015-X

WESTERN ISLAMIC ARCHITECTURE: A Concise Introduction, John D. Hoag. Profusely illustrated critical appraisal compares and contrasts Islamic mosques and palaces—from Spain and Egypt to other areas in the Middle East. 139 illustrations. 128pp. 6 x 9. 0-486-43760-4

CHINESE ARCHITECTURE: A Pictorial History, Liang Ssu-ch'eng. More than 240 rare photographs and drawings depict temples, pagodas, tombs, bridges, and imperial palaces comprising much of China's architectural heritage. 152 halftones, 94 diagrams. 232pp. 10¾ x 9⅞. 0-486-43999-2

THE RENAISSANCE: Studies in Art and Poetry, Walter Pater. One of the most talked-about books of the 19th century, *The Renaissance* combines scholarship and philosophy in an innovative work of cultural criticism that examines the achievements of Botticelli, Leonardo, Michelangelo, and other artists. "The holy writ of beauty."—Oscar Wilde. 160pp. 5⅜ x 8½. 0-486-44025-7

A TREATISE ON PAINTING, Leonardo da Vinci. The great Renaissance artist's practical advice on drawing and painting techniques covers anatomy, perspective, composition, light and shadow, and color. A classic of art instruction, it features 48 drawings by Nicholas Poussin and Leon Battista Alberti. 192pp. 5⅜ x 8½.
0-486-44155-5

THE ESSENTIAL JEFFERSON, Thomas Jefferson, edited by John Dewey. This extraordinary primer offers a superb survey of Jeffersonian thought. It features writings on political and economic philosophy, morals and religion, intellectual freedom and progress, education, secession, slavery, and more. 176pp. 5⅜ x 8½.
0-486-46599-3

WASHINGTON IRVING'S RIP VAN WINKLE, Illustrated by Arthur Rackham. Lovely prints that established artist as a leading illustrator of the time and forever etched into the popular imagination a classic of Catskill lore. 51 full-color plates. 80pp. 8⅜ x 11. 0-486-44242-X

HENSCHE ON PAINTING, John W. Robichaux. Basic painting philosophy and methodology of a great teacher, as expounded in his famous classes and workshops on Cape Cod. 7 illustrations in color on covers. 80pp. 5⅜ x 8½. 0-486-43728-0

CATALOG OF DOVER BOOKS

LIGHT AND SHADE: A Classic Approach to Three-Dimensional Drawing, Mrs. Mary P. Merrifield. Handy reference clearly demonstrates principles of light and shade by revealing effects of common daylight, sunshine, and candle or artificial light on geometrical solids. 13 plates. 64pp. 5⅜ x 8½. 0-486-44143-1

ASTROLOGY AND ASTRONOMY: A Pictorial Archive of Signs and Symbols, Ernst and Johanna Lehner. Treasure trove of stories, lore, and myth, accompanied by more than 300 rare illustrations of planets, the Milky Way, signs of the zodiac, comets, meteors, and other astronomical phenomena. 192pp. 8⅜ x 11. 0-486-43981-X

JEWELRY MAKING: Techniques for Metal, Tim McCreight. Easy-to-follow instructions and carefully executed illustrations describe tools and techniques, use of gems and enamels, wire inlay, casting, and other topics. 72 line illustrations and diagrams. 176pp. 8¼ x 10⅞. 0-486-44043-5

MAKING BIRDHOUSES: Easy and Advanced Projects, Gladstone Califf. Easy-to-follow instructions include diagrams for everything from a one-room house for bluebirds to a forty-two-room structure for purple martins. 56 plates; 4 figures. 80pp. 8¾ x 6⅜. 0-486-44183-0

LITTLE BOOK OF LOG CABINS: How to Build and Furnish Them, William S. Wicks. Handy how-to manual, with instructions and illustrations for building cabins in the Adirondack style, fireplaces, stairways, furniture, beamed ceilings, and more. 102 line drawings. 96pp. 8¾ x 6⅜. 0-486-44259-4

THE SEASONS OF AMERICA PAST, Eric Sloane. From "sugaring time" and strawberry picking to Indian summer and fall harvest, a whole year's activities described in charming prose and enhanced with 79 of the author's own illustrations. 160pp. 8¼ x 11. 0-486-44220-9

THE METROPOLIS OF TOMORROW, Hugh Ferriss. Generous, prophetic vision of the metropolis of the future, as perceived in 1929. Powerful illustrations of towering structures, wide avenues, and rooftop parks–all features in many of today's modern cities. 59 illustrations. 144pp. 8¼ x 11. 0-486-43727-2

THE PATH TO ROME, Hilaire Belloc. This 1902 memoir abounds in lively vignettes from a vanished time, recounting a pilgrimage on foot across the Alps and Apennines in order to "see all Europe which the Christian Faith has saved." 77 of the author's original line drawings complement his sparkling prose. 272pp. 5⅜ x 8½. 0-486-44001-X

THE HISTORY OF RASSELAS: Prince of Abissinia, Samuel Johnson. Distinguished English writer attacks eighteenth-century optimism and man's unrealistic estimates of what life has to offer. 112pp. 5⅜ x 8½. 0-486-44094-X

A VOYAGE TO ARCTURUS, David Lindsay. A brilliant flight of pure fancy, where wild creatures crowd the fantastic landscape and demented torturers dominate victims with their bizarre mental powers. 272pp. 5⅜ x 8½. 0-486-44198-9

Paperbound unless otherwise indicated. Available at your book dealer, online at **www.doverpublications.com**, or by writing to Dept. GI, Dover Publications, Inc., 31 East 2nd Street, Mineola, NY 11501. For current price information or for free catalogs (please indicate field of interest), write to Dover Publications or log on to **www.doverpublications.com** and see every Dover book in print. Dover publishes more than 400 books each year on science, elementary and advanced mathematics, biology, music, art, literary history, social sciences, and other areas.